Childrearing Values in the United States and China

Childrearing Values in the United States and China

A Comparison of Belief Systems and Social Structure

Hong Xiao

PRAEGER

Westport, Connecticut
London

Library of Congress Cataloging-in-Publication Data

Xiao, Hong, 1959–
    Childrearing values in the United States and China : a comparison of belief systems and social structure / Hong Xiao.
        p. cm.
    Includes bibliographical references and index.
    ISBN 0–275–97313–1 (alk. paper)
    1. Child rearing—Social aspects—United States. 2. Child rearing—Social aspects—China. 3. Social values—United States. 4. Social values—China. 5. Social structure—United States. 6. Social structure—China. I. Title.
    HQ769.X53 2001
    649′.173—dc21   00–069271

British Library Cataloguing in Publication Data is available.

Library of Congress Catalog Card Number: 00–069271
ISBN: 0–275–97313–1

First published in 2001

Praeger Publishers, 88 Post Road West, Westport, CT 06881
An imprint of Greenwood Publishing Group, Inc.
www.praeger.com

Printed in the United States of America

The paper used in this book complies with the
Permanent Paper Standard issued by the National
Information Standards Organization (Z39.48–1984).

10 9 8 7 6 5 4 3 2 1

Copyright Acknowledgments

The author and publisher gratefully acknowledge permission for use of the following material:

Chapter 4, "Childrearing Values and Their Predictors: Findings from the U.S. Sample" is based on "Class, Gender, and Parental Values in the 1990s," by Hong Xiao, *Gender & Society* 14(6). Copyright © 2000 Sociologists for Women in Society, with permission of Sage Publications, Inc.

Chapter 5, "Sources of Childrearing Values: Findings from the Chinese Sample" is based on "Structure of Child-rearing Values in Urban China," by Hong Xiao, *Sociological Quarterly* 43(3). With permission of the Pacific Sociological Association and the University of California Press.

Chapter 6, "The United States and China Comparisons" is based on "Independence and Obedience: An Analysis of Child Socialization Values in the United States and China," by Hong Xiao, *Journal of Comparative Family Studies* 30(4). With permission of the *Journal of Comparative Family Studies*, Department of Sociology, The University of Calgary.

To Chenyang, Fay, and Hansen

Contents

List of Tables

Acknowledgments

A book of this nature owes much to many. I am profoundly grateful to my mentors at the University of Connecticut. Nancy Andes and Kenneth Neubeck brought me into the field of sociology. Jane R. Wilkie sustained my endurance in the graduate program. Myra Marx Ferree inspired me to undertake the research and continues to be a model and inspiration.

Many other individuals provided moral and intellectual support while I was completing the research. My deep appreciation is extended to the following people: Marjorie Bond, Deborah Davis, Michael Frank, Zhongxue Gan, Tim Kasser, Mary Ann Lally, Ira Smolensky, and Xiaoshu Zhu. I wish to thank the National Endowment for the Humanities for a summer seminar fellowship support at Columbia University. Discussions with Andrew J. Nathan, director of the seminar, and fellow seminar participants were enlightening. I am equally grateful to the support of many friends from the Central Washington University community. Their words of encouragement and acts of kindness are forever treasured. A sincere thanks is also due to Dr. James Sabin and Nina Duprey of Greenwood Publishing Group for their assistance in the production of the book.

Most special acknowledgment goes to my family. My husband, Chenyang Li, has been my most important source of intellectual as well as personal support. I am thankful for his encouragement, critique, and understanding. My two children, Fay and Hansen, have also given me more support than any mother can expect from children of their ages. I dedicate this book to them.

Chapter 1

Introduction

This book is a study of how social class, gender, and national culture influence childrearing values in the United States and China. As such, it is part of an old and enduring sociological tradition that examines the consequences of class stratification, part of a new and growing feminist scholarship that analyzes the outcomes of gender construction, and part of revitalized and expanding comparative research that tests the generalizability of theories and models in different social-cultural contexts. My main interest is in the psychological effects of social class, gender, and national culture on family life, particularly on childrearing values—characteristics that people value most in children. I examine childrearing values and their determinants in a comparative context.

PURPOSE OF STUDY

This study has three primary purposes. First, it challenges the common claim that childrearing values have a single underlying dimension and that this dimension is primarily related to social class (Alwin 1984, 1989; Gecas 1979; Kohn 1977; Kohn and Schooler 1983; Kohn et al. 1990). Drawing on class–value theory and gender–value theory, it further examines the structure and meanings of childrearing values and argues that childrearing orientations are multidimensional. Besides the widely claimed class–related valuation of autonomy and conformity, there is also a valuation of caring ethics. Second, it investigates the impact of social structure on values in the United States and China. The main issue for the United States is how class and gender intersect in affecting childrearing values. Although both class stratification and gender stratification result in social inequality, the two stratification systems generate different psychological effects on childrearing values. The key question for China is how social stratification shapes values in a command economy. Finally, the study explores universal norms as well as cross-cultural differences in childrearing values. In particular, it seeks to demonstrate how value hierarchies are constructed and shaped in the United States (a Western market economy) and China (an Eastern command economy).

In addressing these questions, this research seeks to add to our understanding of the effects that stratification and culture have on the ways that people act out the roles of parents in two different societies. In exploring and comparing the consequences of stratification on childrearing values in the United States and China, we can better understand if social class and gender exert similar influence on individuals living in distinctive cultures and societies. Findings of the study will enhance our understanding of how the United States and China converge and diverge in the process of status reproduction, an important issue in cross-national/cross-cultural research.

Long-standing class–value theory argues that autonomy and conformity represent two fundamental value orientations in child socialization, and these two value orientations are primarily related to social class. Whereas middle-class parents value more autonomy, working-class parents emphasize more conformity (Alwin 1984, 1989; Gecas 1979; Kohn 1977; Kohn and Schooler 1983). The fundamental importance of these class-specific value orientations, social scientists argue, is that while a valuation of autonomy facilitates children's upward social mobility, a valuation of obedience prohibits it.

In the earlier studies, however, the class position of the man/father was indexed for the entire family. Recent inquiries in the woman/mother's class–value relationship have found that, although women have lower socioeconomic status (measured by a continuous index of educational level and occupational prestige level), they are more likely than men to value children's autonomy (Spade 1991; Wright and Wright 1976; Xiao and Andes 1999). Such findings suggest that the standard class–value model, which is primarily based on men's experience, does not fit when women's childrearing values are considered. Employing a categorical measure of social class, however, the present study finds that women do not uniformly value autonomy more than men do; rather, only women with advantaged positions in the social structure value autonomy more than men do. This finding supports the widely held contention that it generally takes more determination, independence, and imagination (three value items that make up the autonomy value dimension) for professional women to succeed in their occupational positions. Thus, the different occupational experiences of American women and men explain part of the gender gap in the sources of autonomy valuation.

More recently, feminist scholarship challenged the class–value model. Some feminists argued that a gender gap exists in fundamental value orientations. Drawing on the feminist scholarship, the present research further examines the structure of childrearing values and has found that, in addition to the autonomy versus conformity dimension, there is an achievement versus care dimension in childrearing values. Contrary to the arguments of feminist theory, however, in my analysis, the care orientation is not related to gender, nor is it related to parental status or motherhood.

Studies of intergenerational social mobility and status attainment have also found that mechanisms of stratification in China differ very much from those identified in market economies. This study assesses the impact of social class on childrearing values in contemporary urban Chinese families. The findings suggest that while social class is a demarcation in childrearing values in urban China, the class difference deviates from what has been observed in market economies. For example, Chinese foremen and supervisors occupy relatively advantaged positions in the social structure, but they value conformity more and autonomy less than others. This pattern is very surprising and exactly opposite to the class–value theory. I have, however, found logical explanations for this "anomaly." Since the Chinese Communist Party promotes conformity and allocates career opportunities to the loyal, status attainment in China is closely related to political reliability and conformity. As a social group, Chinese foremen/supervisors in my data display the lowest educational attainment and are more likely to have a conventional outlook. The theory of the communist political system suggests that they have achieved career advancement mainly because of political conformity and obedience to authorities (Walder 1985). This suggestion is in line with empirical studies of social mobility in China (Bian 1994; Walder 1995).

Parents also develop their beliefs and perceptions about raising children based on their cultural socialization (Julian et al. 1994; Lee and Zhan 1991). Socialization, the process by which children are educated and/or indoctrinated with the attitudes, values, and behaviors of a society, is an integral part of child rearing in every culture. As the general social structure is influenced by culture, the content of socialization is also based on the salient cultural values of the society. Cultural values and beliefs, in combination with social structure, ultimately influence the kinds of qualities that people consider most desirable and important in children. The United States and China are two societies with distinctive cultures. While American culture is believed to be centered in the values derived from Judeo-Christian roots, Chinese culture is considered to be built upon a value system crystallized in Confucianism (Tu 1990; Wu and Tseng 1985). As such, American culture is said to value individual independence and achievement. Chinese culture, on the other hand, is found to prefer group cohesiveness and social order (Bond 1991; Hsu 1981). With regard to parenting, observers seem to agree that Chinese parents, in the past, were prone to endorse authoritarian parenting orientations disproportionally—that is, to value in children obedience at the expense of independence. However, results from recent studies point to some changes. Contemporary Chinese parents show a low degree of authoritarianism in parent–child relationships (Ho and Kang 1984; Lin and Fu 1990). Some scholars even claim that Chinese parents are behaving more and more like their Western counterparts (Ho 1989). Unfortunately, this claim is based primarily on observations outside mainland China. To date, very little literature systematically compares Chinese and Western childrearing values.

This research contributes to contemporary stratification theory and research in that it combines class theory and the gender perspective in its inquiry into how different stratification systems influence childrearing values. Because life experiences influence values and because both social class and gender condition life experiences, this study argues that gender is as important as social class in explaining value variations.

Furthermore, it is the first study that systematically analyzes the link between social structure and childrearing values in China. It is often believed that Chinese regard childrearing as one of the fundamental issues in their adult lives, and research has documented major changes in Chinese families in recent years, yet little is known about what kinds of qualities Chinese adults desire most in children.

Lastly, the comparative aspect of the analysis is particularly important; it goes beyond the usual single-case study approach to the topic. Previous research on childrearing values has produced a number of generalizations. This study provides an opportunity to test the validity of the generalizations in different social and cultural contexts. Comparisons between the United States and China enhance our knowledge about where the two cultures and social systems converge and diverge. As our world becomes a more global and increasingly interdependent society, knowledge and understanding of other cultures become more vital to success in both competition and cooperation. This study seeks such knowledge.

ORGANIZATION OF THE CHAPTERS

Chapter 2 lays a theoretical foundation for the study. In this chapter, I review research literature on childrearing values and develop my research hypotheses about the nature and the structure of childrearing values and their relationships to social class, gender, and national culture in the two countries. Specifically, I examine the structure and meanings of childrearing values in light of class–value theory, gender-value theory, and culture-value theory. I also hypothesize how social stratification based on class, gender, and race and cultural traditions conditions people's value systems and thus affects the process of social mobility in market and command economies.

Data, methods, and data analysis strategies are the contents of Chapter 3. Using data from the World Values Survey, I construct three childrearing value scales for the United States and China separately. They are valuation of autonomy, valuation of conformity, and valuation of caring ethics. The contents of the three value scales of each country show both universal norms as well as national differences in the structure of childrearing values in the United States and China.

Chapter 4 contains data analyses in the United States. These analyses examine the relationships among the three childrearing values and a host of socioeconomic factors. The findings elucidate the complex nature of belief systems, while highlighting the effects of social class, gender, and race on childrearing values.

Chapter 5 focuses on social stratification systems and childrearing values in China. Given that mechanisms of social mobility in command economies vary from those identified in market economies, my analyses seek to identify how the Chinese command economy shapes value orientations. Indeed, the patterns revealed in China deviate from what has been observed in the United States. Among others factors, social class, age, and family structure exert great influence on Chinese childrearing values.

Chapter 6 takes a macro level approach and compares, side by side, the patterns of childrearing values of the United States and China. Since the two countries differ very much in cultural traditions, political systems, and economic development, I address two major issues in this chapter. First I seek to demonstrate where and how Americans and Chinese differ in their orientations toward children. Second, I seek to explain the national differences by probing into the sources of value variations in the two countries.

The final chapter, Chapter 7, summarizes the major findings. Implications of the findings are discussed in the context of cultural traditions, political economic systems, and social changes. It also addresses the limitations of the study and offers directions for future research.

Chapter 2

Childrearing Values of Americans and Chinese: Expectations from the Literature

VALUES AND CHILDREARING VALUES

The concept of value has been defined in many different ways. The phenomena that it covers range from specific beliefs such as religious or political ideologies to general life orientations. What are values? Perhaps because the word "value" is a highly abstract concept, there is no common definition of values among scholars. Over the years, various kinds of definitions have been offered; some are simplistic, and others are quite complex. In simplistic definitions a value has been defined as being equivalent to a worldview (Redfield 1953), a cultural theme (Opler 1954), a way of life (Morris 1956), or a criterion for preference or justification for behavior (Williams 1968, 1970). In complex definitions a value has been defined as "any element, common to a series of situations, which is capable of evoking an overt response in the individual" (Linton, 1945: 111) or "a conception, explicit or implicit, distinctive of an individual or characteristic of a group, of the desirable which influences the selection from available modes, means, and ends of action" (Kluckhohn 1951: 395). It has also been defined as "an enduring belief that a specific mode or end-state of existence is preferable to an opposite or converse mode of conduct or end-state of existence" (Rokeach 1973: 5).

Many others share to some degree Rokeach's (1973) definition of values. Researchers seem to agree upon the following characteristics of values: (1) values are intangible; they are theoretical constructs or concepts; (2) they are more abstract than attitudes in the sense that they transcend specific objects, events, and situations; (3) they function as evaluative criteria, representing desirable or desired outcomes or behaviors; (4) they are systems organized hierarchically with degrees of importance and priority; (5) they are products of socialization and are linked to the affective system; and (6) they have some stability, but the importance of particular values may change with life experiences and with the emergence of new roles and responsibilities (Feather 1994; Kahle and Timmer 1983; Rokeach and Ball-Rokeach 1989; Schwartz 1992; Schwartz and Huismans 1995).

Along this line of thinking, Kohn (1977) considers values to be "standards of desirability" and "criteria of preference." According to Kohn (1977: 18), childrearing (or parental) values are the characteristics that parents "consider most desirable to inculcate in their children." The present study adopts Kohn's definition and conceptualizes childrearing values as the characteristics or qualities of children desirable to parents.

DIMENSIONS OF CHILDREARING VALUES

Most research on childrearing values has been undertaken in Western nations, particularly in the United States. Kohn's (1977) work is the most influential. Using a 1964 National Opinion Research Center (NORC) sample survey of fathers of children aged 3 to 15, Kohn analyzed the relationship between social class (primarily occupation), and the attributes that parents value in their children. In the survey, the respondents were asked to choose from a set of 13 items the three most desirable qualities as well as the one most desirable. In addition, they were asked to choose the three least desirable traits as well as the one least desirable. A factor analysis of the 13 value items generated two statistically significant factors. Kohn, however, focused his analyses on only one factor because he found this factor significantly related to social class. This factor is identified as "self-direction versus conformity" (Kohn 1977: 57). The items that have positive loadings (e.g., that the child is considerate of others, is interested in how and why things happen, is responsible, and has good sense and sound judgment) are said to reflect values toward self-direction. The items that have negative loadings (e.g., that the child has good manners, is neat and clean, and obeys his or her parents well) reflect values toward conformity. Kohn argues that there is a major difference between self-direction and conformity; while the former refers to internal standards for behavior, the latter refers to externally imposed rules. This argument, in concert with his factor analysis results, leads to his conceptualization of a single value dimension in parental values, with conformity and autonomy representing the opposite ends of the same continuum. The argument of the unidimensionality of parental values has been supported and sustained in subsequent comparative work carried out by Kohn and his colleagues (Kohn et al. 1986, 1990).

Influenced by Kohn's (1977) work, virtually all of the studies on child socialization center on the discussion and analysis of the self-direction/autonomy versus conformity/obedience differences (Alwin 1986, 1988, 1989; Ellis et al. 1978; Ellis and Petersen 1992; Luster et al. 1989; Spade 1991). However, many do so without even examining the meaning and the nature of a given set of parental value items. They assume that parental values represent mainly two values—autonomy and conformity—and that these two values are the end points of a single bipolar dimension. The traditional argument is that if parents differ in the kinds of qualities that they consider important/desirable in children, the main difference lies in their valuation of autonomy versus conformity.

In the few studies that attempt to replicate Kohn's single-value dimension measure, the results are inconsistent. Spade (1991), for example, is able to identify one dimension with two poles through a confirmatory factor analysis of 12 value items. But the data on which Spade's analysis is based come from a relatively small middle-class sample (n = 186 dual-worker families) and are limited racially (including only whites) and geographically (drawn from a suburban area in upstate New York).

Other efforts of replication have been generally unsatisfactory, however. Using data from the 1973 NORC General Social Survey, Wright and Wright (1976) sought to replicate and extend Kohn's (1977) model. The 12 value items used in the General Social Survey are identical to those used in Kohn's research, but Wright and Wright were unable to duplicate a self-direction factor equivalent to that of Kohn's. Some of the differences in measurement and sampling procedures observed by Wright and Wright may explain the failure of a replication. First, there is a difference in the specific focus of the value items in the two studies. In the 1973 NORC General Social Survey, the value items ask about a child in general, whereas Kohn's questions ask about the respondent's own child or children of a specific age and sex. Second, there is a sampling difference. Kohn's study is based on a nationally representative sample of employed fathers, whereas the Wrights' replication is based on males from a nationally representative sample of households.[1] Not all men in the Wrights' sample are fathers; instead, men are included who were living in households where there were children.

Third, Kohn's original study analyzes fathers of children ages 3 to 15, whereas the Wrights' study analyzes respondents living with children aged 0 to 17. Only when the Wrights run a factor analysis on 7 out of the 12 value items, could they replicate the self-direction factor identified by Kohn.

The replication attempts by others have also met with some difficulties. Sometimes a given set of parental value items does not show any meaningful latent dimensions (Ifcic 1993). Other times data yield two distinct factors. While one factor clearly reflects conformity, the other is not reflective of autonomy valuation. In addition, the items with the most face validity regarding an autonomy value do not cluster together within a factor analysis framework (Biblarz 1993). At still other times the autonomy factor can be statistically identified, but it is not correlated to socioeconomic status (Krosnick and Alwin 1988). Certainly, the findings that do not match those reported by Kohn and his colleagues are not rare, yet they have so far received only limited attention in socialization research. These findings provide some basis for challenging the unidimensionality of parental values and the opposing nature of autonomy and conformity values.

Scholars studying values have long argued that values are complex and multifaceted. Empirical research in political science and psychology postulates that people's beliefs and value orientations are structured along multiple dimensions. A substantial body of evidence also suggests that value orientations are rooted in social experiences and that an individual's proclivity toward a particular value is related to a variety of factors (Rokeach 1973; Schwartz 1992). Among the major factors, social class is considered particularly closely linked to parental valuation of autonomy and conformity. The association between people's position in a social stratification system and their emphasis on characteristics related to autonomy and conformity is perhaps the best-documented relationship. Studies over the past several decades have found that, while middle-class parents place greater emphasis on their children's autonomy, working-class parents are more concerned with their children's conformity (Alwin 1989; Kohn 1977; Miller and Swanson 1958).

Contemporary United States is, however, stratified not only by social class but also by gender. Gender theory argues that the different roles assigned women and men have pervasive effects on the ways that women and men think and behave. Some recent feminist scholarship suggests that women and men do not develop their value orientations and moral reasoning along the same continuum (Gilligan 1982). Gender gaps have been found, among other things, in attitudes toward work values, in care-taking behaviors, and in religious involvement. In general, women are found to be more likely than men to be in jobs that involve helping others, to express other-oriented concerns, to emphasize the importance of religion, and to be active in religious participation (Batson et al. 1993; Beutel and Marini 1995; Marini et al. 1996; Miller and Hofmann 1995).

If people's values for children are reflective of values for themselves and if values are linked to different dimensions in the social stratification system, it is conceivable that parental values are multifaceted. The preceding literature review suggests the following hypothesis about the nature and the structure of childrearing values in the United States: characteristics that people desire in children are not organized along a single value continuum with two poles of autonomy and conformity; in addition to the valuation of autonomy and conformity, childrearing values may have embedded in them other latent clusters/dimensions of values such as care-oriented values.

NATIONAL CULTURE AND VALUE STRUCTURE

Some research in other national cultures has failed to confirm that adults differ on a common set of values that they consider important for children (Ma and Smith 1990), although the support for the argument in cross-national investigations is often reported by Kohn and his colleagues (Kohn et al. 1986; 1990). Due to the influence of national culture, characteristics considered valuable/desirable in one society may not be thought so in another society. The frequent failures to replicate value constructs generated in U.S.-based studies in other regions and countries suggest that the meanings and the structure of values vary by culture (Bond 1988; Smith and Bond 1993; Smith and Dugan 1996).

A fundamental reason for the variation of values is that values are deeply rooted in ideology. The discussion of the valuation of conformity and autonomy occupies a central place in the U.S. child socialization literature. This is partly due to the influence of the meritocracy ideology that dominates the American society. This ideology emphasizes self-reliance and individual responsibility and dictates that individuals are personally responsible for their own progress—or lack of it—in the social hierarchy. People are presumed to have the freedom to do so. The pursuit of individual happiness and success is seen as the primary endeavor of life. Hence, autonomy is praised, while obedience is less valued. The concerns raised in the United States by the studies of conformity and autonomy, then, seem to reflect the norms of American society.

In China, self-help and self-reliance are also much emphasized. However, the primary purpose of the emphasis is not to pursue personal happiness and success but rather to contribute to the glory of the family and the well-being of the society. Thus, autonomy may not be so distinct from conformity. I argue that the nature and structure of parental values may differ by national culture. In other words, the value constructs/clusters found in the United States may not be identical to those found in mainland China. Furthermore, even when Americans and Chinese show similar patterns in their parental value selections, the roots of their thinking may differ.

CLASS AND VALUES IN THE UNITED STATES

Empirical research in the United States has documented an enduring relationship between social class and childrearing values: working-class parents are more concerned with their children's conformity, while middle-class parents value more their children's self-direction. While Kohn's (1981) work is best known in the area, other studies have arrived at similar conclusions: working-class parents are more "restrictive," and middle-class parents are more "permissive" (Bronfenbrenner 1958); working-class parents emphasize "obedience," while middle-class parents emphasize "autonomy" in their children (Alwin 1988); working-class parents are characterized by "traditional conceptions," while middle-class parents are characterized by "developmental conceptions" of childrearing (Duvall 1946); working-class parents have "bureaucratic" orientations, while middle-class parents have "entrepreneurial" orientations (Miller and Swanson 1958). Work in this field has progressed from descriptions to explanations, a progression earmarked by the work of Kohn and his colleagues (Kohn 1977; Kohn and Schooler 1983).

In explaining what it is about class that makes the difference, researchers (Kohn 1977; Kohn and Schooler 1983; Mortimer 1974) concentrate on occupation as the most salient aspect of social class. They argue that work in blue-collar occupations is typically closely supervised, lacks complexity, and is highly routinized. Success in these jobs is largely defined by following rules. In white-collar occupations, success is achieved largely by virtue of individual initiative and self-reliance. This difference in occupational conditions gives rise to certain adaptive values and affects people's perception of the society they live in, and this difference in adaptive values affects their childrearing orientations.

Why should people's work conditions affect their values for children? In other words, why do individuals who are closely supervised at work and engage in substantively simple, repetitive work day in and day out value conformity to external authority, and why do individuals who exercise greater control over their work conditions value autonomy for children? The explanatory model developed by Kohn (1977) proposes that individuals' social class or socioeconomic status determines how much self-direction they can exercise in their work. Occupational self-direction refers to the degree to which individuals are free in the work setting to control their activity and to escape external sources of control, for example, machines and supervisory personnel. The on-the-job occupational conditions that determine occupational self-direction, in turn, influence off-the-job values.

In his interpretation of the influence of work on childrearing values, Kohn reasons that through exposure to various conditions of work, people learn about the kinds of personal characteristics that are required for job performance, security, and success in their particular work worlds. In working-class jobs, the kinds of traits required are more likely to involve following rules to the fullest, adapting to a pace defined by others or by machinery, and conforming to external authority. In middle-class jobs, the kinds of traits required are more likely to involve the use of one's own judgment and the ability to make decisions in complex work situations. The argument is that people, in part through their own occupational experiences, learn about those characteristics that are required to get along in work and perhaps in the larger society. The valuation of autonomy or conformity is, then, a response to the nature and structure of work.

Kohn's measures of parents' social class were originally based on men's education and occupational experience. Later studies by Kohn and his colleagues have included women's social status and occupational experience and obtained findings that are consistent for women as well as men. However, the effects of occupational conditions on parental values are more notable for their ubiquity than for their strength (Dimaggio 1994). In general, the effects are statistically significant but relatively small. These studies tell us little about the factors that may account for the variance in parental values that work content does not explain. Additionally, the class–value relationship is not as strong for women as for men (Kohn et al. 1986).

Other studies using different samples and/or different methodologies provide mixed support for the class–value theory. Wright and Wright (1976), for example, tested the theory in their analysis of the NORC General Social Survey data. The results of multiple regression analysis for both fathers and mothers are parallel to earlier findings; that is, parents' class locations influence their valuation of self-direction versus conformity for children. However, Wright and Wright found that analyses centering on social class (and occupation) overlook two-fifths to three-fifths of the explainable variance in parental valuation of self-direction. The addition of region, race, religion, religious attendance, ethnicity, and city size contributes between a third and a half of the total variance explainable by the model. Others have also documented the effects of nonclass variables on childrearing values (Burns et al. 1984; Julian et al. 1994). In a study using the cumulative NORC General Social Survey data, Davis (1982) examines the consequences of stratification for attitudes. He finds that the associations between stratification measures and answers to 49 attitude questions vary; some are robust, and some are weak. These findings cast doubt on the assumption that people's attitudes arise mechanically and solely from their locations in a class-based order.

Of particular importance in more recent literature is the discovery that there is a persistent gender gap in childrearing values. That is, women tend to value autonomy in children more than men do. Men, on the other hand, are more likely than women to stress conformity (Xiao and Andes 1999). Gender also interferes with the effect of class on values. In her analysis of socialization values of white married couples, Spade (1991) examined the husband's as well as the wife's social positions and their valuation of self-direction for children. She found that women are more likely to value self-direction for children than men despite their lower occupational status, education, income, and occupational self-direction.

How can we explain and understand this gender difference? Social psychology theory and feminist theory on women's roles in the family suggest two contrasting answers. Social psychologists have suggested that people tend to desire and value what they don't have. In American society, females are taught to be more submissive, passive, obedient, and nurturing than are males. These traits and their gender put women in a less advantaged position in labor market competition. In addition, women's overall lower income makes them more likely to depend on others. Compared with men, women tend to feel that they have less control in their lives than do men. A sense of lack of control may prompt women to believe that it is important to be autonomous. Thus, they value autonomy in children more than men do.

Feminist theory, on the other hand, may offer an entirely different explanation that emphasizes the influence of feminism on women's roles in the family. Feminism is both an ideology and a movement. As an ideology, it is a framework for interpreting gender issues that grew out of the contemporary women's movement. In most accounts, feminism involves a strong commitment to the democratic values of freedom, autonomy, and equality (Clement 1996; Dietz 1985). As a movement, its main goal is to end gender inequality. In the course of the twentieth century, feminism caused shock waves in virtually every social institution. One of the most significant changes is in the attitude toward women's roles in the family. Traditionally, a woman/wife/mother's primary responsibility was to her family, husband, and children. Today, however, more than two-thirds of the married couples in American have dual-earner marriages. Although both men and women support female employment, women, because of their gender and relatively disadvantaged position in social structure, are more likely than men to have positive attitudes toward women's labor force participation (Herring and Wilson-Sadberry 1993; Spade 1994). Since employed women are more likely than nonemployed women to be economically independent, it is then conceivable that a positive attitude towards women's labor force participation may generate a preference for autonomy.

Undoubtedly, existing literature suggests that there is a gender difference in the relationship between social class and childrearing values. Kohn's class–value model, derived only from men's experience, is clearly inadequate in explaining the difference. However, in these studies, there is no categorical distinction among women and men on their class identities. Social class is measured by a continuous index of educational level and occupational prestige level. Thus, it is unclear whether women of all classes uniformly value autonomy more than men do.

Social scientists also challenge the magnitude and stability of class differences in childrearing values. They argue that, accompanied by demographic, social, and cultural changes that occurred during the past decades, American families and the relationships between parents and their children have undergone substantial changes. In contemporary American families, there is a movement from a traditional patriarchal structure toward a more democratic and less authoritarian one (Cherlin 1999; Margolis 1998). Using survey data from the Detroit metropolitan area obtained in 1958, 1971, and 1983, Alwin (1984) reports consistent increases over this time period in the valuation of autonomy for children and a decrease in valuation of obedience to authority. Other studies have also observed changes in Americans' attitudes and orientations to the family (Alwin 1988, 1989; Glenn 1988; Wilkie 1993).

Thus, two recurrent findings coexist in the study of the effects of social class on childrearing values. The first shows that social class, mainly through occupational experiences, has a pervasive impact on parental values. This finding draws primarily on earlier data and is supported largely by Kohn and his colleagues. The second finding, based on more recent data, suggests a decline in the importance of social class in stressing autonomy or conformity in children. Time differences of the data sets may explain some of the inconsistencies in findings. Today, parents clearly have become more concerned with children's development than before. Furthermore, during the past two decades, many changes in the nature of work have occurred because of technological advances in computers and telecommunications. The emergence of information technologies has brought about highly automated production systems. These systems often require higher levels of skill for normal operation, even of workers who are relatively low in the organization hierarchy (Adler 1986; Crouter and Manker 1994; Thomas 1993). These changes made it increasingly difficult to draw the line between manual and nonmanual jobs. While these studies do not always focus on the effects of social class on childrearing values, their results are often interpreted by others to mean that, over the past two decades, working conditions have become generally similar for manual and nonmanual workers. Occupational autonomy appears to have become increasingly unimportant in shaping socialization values.

GENDER AND CARE-ORIENTED VALUES

Social scientists are also divided on whether there are gender differences in fundamental value orientations. Theories of gender argue that the distinctive male and female roles shape people's understanding of the world. As a result, women and men do not develop their value orientations along the same continuum (Gilligan 1982). Specifically, feminist morality theory and research have documented a competition/achievement versus care/affiliation dimension in value orientations. While these two orientations are not wholly gender-specific, they are strongly related to gender. It is proposed that men and women differ in their orientations, with men emphasizing competition and women preferring care in relationships (Gilligan and Attanucci 1988; Eisenberg et al. 1989; Sochting et al. 1994).

Because human values function as guiding principles in daily life, some feminists claim, gender differences in thinking and behavior result from these gender-based value orientations. Some empirical research shows that women/girls are more likely than men/boys to be care-oriented and to express concern and responsibility for the well-being of others (Beutel and Marini 1995; Belansky and Boggiano 1994). Gender gaps have also been found, among other things, in attitudes toward work values and in caretaking behavior. In general, women are more likely than men to be in jobs that involve helping others and express other-oriented concerns (Beutel and Marini 1995; Marini et al. 1996).

Some of the gender differences in value orientations are also evident in research demonstrating gender gaps in attitudes toward social collectivities and public policy preferences. Women are more likely than men to express concern and responsibility for the well-being of others (Beutel and Marini 1995; Marini 1990). Women are also more supportive than men of education, health programs, social welfare, and reconciliation and peace (Conover and Sapiro 1993; Eagly 1987; Schlozman et al. 1995; Shapiro and Mahajan 1986). Other evidence shows that women are more extensively involved in caregiving than men in both the home and the workplace. Women are the primary providers of social emotional support in the home (House et al. 1988; Rossi and Rossi 1991) and are more likely to aspire to, and be employed in, jobs that require interpersonal skills and the provision of social-emotional support (England et al. 1994; Marini 1990). Research on work values also shows that women attach more importance than men to jobs that are worthwhile to society and involve helping others (Marini et al. 1996; Mason 1994).

These indications of women's orientation toward caring, unselfishness, respect, and responsibility for others are consistent with the roles normatively prescribed for women. These roles promote the norm of nurturance and care. Society expects women to be self-sacrificing by placing more importance on other people's needs than on their own needs and aiding others in attaining their goals.

Systematic analyses of helping behavior have focused on gender differences in the nature and the types of help that men and women demonstrate. The results indicate that women are not uniformly the more helpful sex but, rather, that they help in different ways than do men. Male helping involves heroic and chivalrous behavior, including nonroutine and risky acts of rescuing others and behavior that shows courtesy and protectiveness of subordinates. While these behaviors occur in relationships with strangers as well as in close relationships, they often focus on short-term encounters and are directed toward women (Eagly 1987). Women, on the other hand, tend to help in a nurturing way and provide emotional support, especially when their helping is aimed at family members and close friends (Belansky and Boggiano 1994; Vaux 1985).

The view that women and men specialize in gender-specific value orientations has not gone unchallenged. Some studies found no gender differences in moral judgments or value orientations—women are just as capable as men of being competition-oriented (Cohn 1991; Walker 1984, 1986). Other investigations show that gender differences are generally inconsistent and conditional on people's specific life circumstance (Hyde and Plant 1995; Prince-Gibson and Schwartz 1998). Whether women and men consistently differ in value orientations certainly needs further investigation. This study continues the exploration of the topic and investigates gender differences in childrearing values.

Some recent feminist theorists have shifted the focus from sex and gender per se to the particular experiences of women and men, especially the experiences of parenting and mothering. They argue that women differ from men in their value orientations not because of their gender but because of their status of being mothers (Bassin et al. 1994). Particularly relevant is the discussion of maternal thinking that emerges from the practice of mothering (Ruddick 1989). The practice of mothering means being primarily responsible for nurturing, protecting, and caring for children. In principle, both men and women can be "mothers." But in reality, most "mothers" are women (Ruddick 1989). Since people who do more parenting and mothering tend to be more caring, more pacifist, and more likely to express concern and responsibility for the well-being of others and since most "mothers" are women, gender differences in values emerge (Conover and Sapiro 1993; Ruddick 1989).

Hence, the feminist literature suggests the following two hypotheses. Gender is centrally related to care-oriented values. Women are more likely than men to endorse in children care-oriented values. In addition, the status of parenthood mediates the effects of gender on childrearing values. Parents, especially those who do the primary parenting— typically mothers—tend to value care-related values more than others.

Little systematic information has been available that bears directly on whether men and women differ in care-oriented values in child socialization. This is because, in the past several decades, studies of childrearing values have focused primarily on class differences in values. Because child socialization plays a significant role in status attainment and because men and women do not share child-care responsibility equally, whether men and women differ in childrearing values should be an important question in sociology of the family and social stratification.

RELIGIOSITY AND CHILDREARING VALUES

My goal here is to assess the relationship between religious involvement and childrearing values. Consideration of religious involvement is particularly important when juxtaposed against the structural variables discussed earlier. I will make a comparison of the roles of structural influences versus cultural ones in determining childrearing values for children.

Much has been written about the association between religion and parental values and/or childrearing practices. Survey research by Lenski (1963) and Alwin (1986) finds that Catholics and Protestants in the United States showed significant differences in parenting and in values that they consider most important in children. Catholics endorsed more authoritarian parenting norms and valued obedience more than Protestants did. Although the differences between Catholics and Protestants in parenting have been diminishing since the 1980s, the influence of religiosity on values and attitudes is still widely observed (Beutel and Marini 1995; Ellison and Sherkat 1993; Schwartz and Huismans 1995).

People who attend church frequently (Kohn 1977) and participate in church activities frequently (Alwin 1986) are more likely to value conformity in children, independently of social class. I examine the effect of religious involvement because every major religion preaches conformity and conventionality. I expect that the level of religiosity/religious participation is positively related to people's valuation of conformity in children.

RACE AND CHILDREARING VALUES

In a recent study, variations in parenting attitudes and behaviors were reported for Caucasian, African American, Hispanic American, and Asian American parents (Julian et al. 1994). African and Hispanic Americans value conformity in children more than do whites. A sizable proportion of this gap may be explained by nonwhite/white differences in the determinants of childrearing values. Drawing from previous research, I have argued that people's social class, level of education, and religiosity, in various ways, significantly impact the kinds of values that they have for children. Nonwhites, on average, are more likely than whites to be located in less advantaged social positions, to have lower levels of education, and to be more religious. Thus, I expect that social class and other relevant variables explain the childrearing values of racial/ethnic minorities as well as they explain the childrearing values of whites. However, given the unique difficulties that racial/ethnic minorities face in a society where racism and discrimination exist, I expect that nonwhites attach greater importance to conformity in children than whites when other factors are taken into account. A greater value for conformity could be understood as a means to prepare children to live in an environment of subtle to overt racism (Peters 1988). For racial minority parents, behavioral conformity among children may lessen their chances of being hurt in social, psychological, and even physical ways.

SOCIAL CLASS AND CHILDREARING VALUES IN CHINA

Studies on childrearing values have been undertaken primarily in the market economy or capitalist societies. With the exception of Kohn et al. (1990), empirical research linking class and childrearing values has focused mainly on capitalist societies such as the United States, Italy, Australia, Japan, and Taiwan. In a rare research comparing stratification systems in both capitalist and socialist, Western and Eastern societies, Kohn and his colleagues (1990) examined childrearing values in the United States, Japan, and Poland. Of particular importance in the comparative studies is the type of society with which the United States is compared. Poland was a socialist society at the time of the survey, and Japan is an Eastern nation. They found that in all three societies social class is consistently related to values. Men who are high in the social order are more likely to value self-direction for children than men who are lower in the social order. Other empirical investigations of non-Western market economies (because data on command economies are scarce) reported similar findings (Ellis et al. 1978; Ellis and Petersen 1992; Ho and Kang 1984; Kohn et al. 1986; Ma and Smith 1993; Olsen 1973, 1975). The implication to be drawn from these studies is that the class-linked valuation of autonomy and conformity is a common phenomenon associated with all cultures and all political economies.

I argue that the structure of childrearing values differs in the market and the command economy. It is true that in all economies childrearing values are shaped by the individual's social position and by the influence of the social milieu, but each political economy evokes a set of mechanisms that condition the status attainment process. In the market economy, education and occupation determine one's position in social structure. While years of schooling may not be perfectly related to occupational achievement and earnings, the impact of education on status attainment is consistent and significant. Better-educated individuals are more likely to move up in the occupational hierarchy and pay scale. In a command economy such as China, the central government controls the allocation of labor and material resources. Government policies, rather than market forces, determine occupational opportunities and reward structures. In such a society, the redistribution system gives rise to different mechanisms of stratification.

Much has been written in recent years on social structure and status attainment in China. Literature on intergenerational mobility suggests that mechanisms of stratification in China differ very much from those identified in market societies. For instance, occupational mobility and earnings depend as much on educational credentials as on political loyalty (Walder 1995; Xie and Hannum 1996). Access to education is often influenced by state policies, and superb education may sometimes lead to downward occupational mobility (Davis 1992). Furthermore, entrance into job sectors, rather than the job per se, constitutes the primary goal of status attainment (Lin and Bian 1991). Thus, it is reasonable to hypothesize that education and occupation exhibit different and inconsistent influence on childrearing values in China's unique political and social context.

Despite its importance in social mobility theory, the structure of childrearing values has received little attention in the literature on status attainment in the Chinese context. While recent research has documented China's distinctive social mobility patterns, there is little investigation on the psychological consequences of the stratification system. Childrearing values influence not only people's behaviors in raising children (Bronfenbrenner 1958; Kohn 1977) but also children's destination in the social structure (Mortimer 1974; Rossi and Rossi 1991). Therefore, an examination of the structure of childrearing values enhances our understanding of the process of status reproduction in socialist China.

To the best of my knowledge, this is the first study that examines the links between social structure and childrearing values in China. Drawing upon findings of social mobility in China, I hypothesize that the effects of social class and education on childrearing values are not as strong as those observed in the United States.

GENDER AND SOCIAL CHANGES

Traditional China is known for its patriarchal family system. All agrarian civilizations rest on patriarchal familial foundations (Stacey 1983). Few patriarchal systems developed to the stage of the hegemony that Confucianism achieved in imperial China. Chinese patriarchy shaped the structure of authority and control of property in the Chinese family. In this system, women's situations were most pitiable. We have heard much about the plight of girls in traditional China who might be killed at birth by parents who did not need another daughter, who could be sold at a very young age as servants, who had to marry whomever their fathers ordered them to marry, and who had no legal rights to property.

In the traditional Chinese society, a person's role was clearly defined by gender. Men occupied a higher class position than women did. Fathers possessed the most dominant role in the family. The father's sphere of responsibility was mainly outside the home, whereas the mother's was inside the home (Abbott et al. 1992; Wang 1990). Raising children was one of the mother's main activities. In childrearing, the mother was supposed to provide loving care and nurturance, and the father was to educate and enforce discipline (Ho 1986).

During the past several decades, the social and cultural contexts in China, especially in urban areas, have changed significantly. The changes in cultural values and gender roles are specially related to the present study. Since the turn of the century, the influence of Confucianism, patriarchy, and traditional culture in urban China has been declining. This is due partly to the impact of several campaigns attacking Confucian doctrines and partly to social and economic transformation (Cheng 1987; Smith 1991). Since the founding of the People's Republic of China in 1949, certain aspects and rituals in Confucianism have been further rejected in China. The communist government denounced Confucianism for providing the ethical rationale for a system of feudalism and patriarchy. Since 1949, the Chinese Communist Party (thereafter CCP) has been the only ruling party in China. The country has been governed according to Chinese communist/socialist ideology. Such ideology permeates every sector of human functioning, including dictating desirable values and attitudes for adults and children. Hence, the CCP's mandates may take precedence over other cultural traditions and Confucianism in shaping Chinese individuals' value orientations, including their socialization ideals for the next generation.

This is not to say that every Chinese is equally influenced by the CCP's ideology. In fact, the CCP's doctrines are not quite consistent over the three periods in the short history of the People's Republic of China. During the first period, the postliberation (1949–1966), the CCP established a strong political order and an effective administrative apparatus. The victory of the communists marked an end to decades of chaos in the country. The majority of the Chinese people were supportive of the new government and willing to cooperate in building a new economy. The political socialization of the time emphasized the spirit of collectivism and loyalty to the CCP. A good example of this emphasis could be observed from the way people were urged to set their priorities: "revolution first, work first, and others first" (Lee and Zhan 1991).

The onset of the Cultural Revolution marked the beginning of the second period (1966–1976). Mao Tse-tung and his followers believed that a new revolutionary movement was necessary to eliminate capitalist elements in the CCP. This was a period of political, economic, and social turmoil in China. The whole nation fell into chaos. The government and other social institutions stopped functioning. Virtually all pre–Cultural Revolution standards of social behavior were heavily criticized. Citizens, especially youth, were encouraged to rebel (Gao 1987).

The third, or the post–Cultural Revolution period (1976–present), started when the Party declared that the Cultural Revolution was over. This move came after Mao's death and the purge of the Gang of Four— the four radical leftist leaders. Political and social order was gradually restored in the country. In an effort to rebuild the Chinese economy and to restore people's confidence and hope in the system, economic reform was initiated in the late 1970s. Since then the country has been increasingly exposed to an influx of Western ideas and advanced technology. It has been speculated that, under the influence of Western thinking, many young Chinese may have become very much westernized. In other words, they may stress independence and individualism more than interdependence and collectivism.

It should be noted that Confucianism and Chinese communist ideology are not totally at odds with each other. In fact, the latter is much influenced by the former. In the ruling ideology of CCP, the society is viewed as a large family, the maintenance of which depends on each individual's contribution. China is said to be a classless society in the sense that no person is better than any other in social ranking. Each individual is a full member of the big family; therefore, each member has the social responsibility of serving and cooperating with other members toward shared goals. At the same time, the party is unambiguous on the importance of hierarchy. The basic rule of party discipline holds that the individual is subordinate to the majority and that the lower level is subordinate to the higher level in the organizational structure (Pye 1984). To examine the education themes in the two social systems, Solomon (1965) compared school textbooks approved by the early republican government of 1922 and by the People's Republic of China in 1960. The comparisons show that the theme of emphasizing conformity and loyalty did not change much in four decades, although some differences are noticeable; the primary social loyalty shifted from family to the nation and the Communist Party, and the sense of social responsibility was much more emphasized. The most obvious change was that the roles of women became much more active in the postrevolution textbooks.

Since 1949, women's liberation had been one of the major themes in a series of campaigns. By 1990 not only was China one of the leading societies in female workforce participation, but the earning differential between male and female workers was one of the smallest among industrialized nations (Bonney et al. 1992; Hsieh and Burgess 1994). With women's greater participation in the workforce and greater contribution to family income, men were assuming a greater role in parenting and domestic chores (Abbott et al. 1992). A time budget study of 2,293 workers in two northeastern cities of China showed a greater degree of equal sharing in housework than was the case in Russia, Czechoslovakia, France, and the United States (Wang and Li 1982). While Chinese husbands, on the average, shared more than two-fifths (43%) of the total housework time with their wives each day, husbands in the other countries shared approximately one-fourth (21.1%–28.6%) of the daily housework time.

Bonney et al. (1992) compared urban working-class samples from China, Japan, and Great Britain. China was found to have greater sharing of domestic chores between marital partners than were Japan and Great Britain. For the tasks of washing up, cleaning the house, doing laundry, and cooking, the percentages of exclusively wife's responsibility ranged from 35 percent to 47 percent in China. By comparison, these figures ranged from 53 percent to 94 percent in Britain and are above 89 percent for all the chores in Japan. Whereas less than 5 percent of the husbands entirely or mainly performed the four chores in Britain and Japan, 9 percent to 20 percent of the husbands in China took principal responsibility for these tasks.

If the content of socialization is based on the salient cultural values and is linked to the general social context in a society, the changes in cultural values and gender roles should be reflected in people's childrearing orientations. Thus, I hypothesize that controlling for other structural variables, gender exerts little effect on the kind of qualities that Chinese consider important in children.

CROSS - NATIONAL COMPARISONS

Little systematic information has been available that bears directly on where the United States and China, as two different national cultures, converge and diverge in the kinds of characteristics considered most important in children. However, the preceding discussion is helpful in developing expectations about Americans and Chinese preferences of child socialization values at a national level. In addition, there is some evidence in empirical comparative studies about differences between Americans and Chinese, including Chinese residing outside mainland China, with respect to cultural values and childrearing practices. The empirical studies related to differences in cultural values and the discussions in the previous sections of this research can provide the basis for hypothesizing about cross-cultural differences in American and Chinese socialization ideals for children.

There have been numerous discussions of typical American values. Common to many of the discussions of distinctive American values is the perception that Americans value self-governance and individual independence, are ambivalent toward authority, and admire those who achieve by their own efforts (Feather 1975; Hofstede 1980; Rokeach 1968, 1973; Triandis 1995). Hofstede (1980) found the United States to be the most individualistic culture. American economic and political systems promote individual rewards for individual effort. Among the factors that may have been responsible for the individualistic belief system are classical liberalism, affluence, the open frontier, and social and geographic mobility. Others attribute the individualistic tendency, in part, to the early upper-class settlers, including the writers of the U.S. Constitution and other early leaders (Fliegelman 1993; Triandis 1995). They argue that the early leaders set the tone of what was acceptable behavior in North America. Additionally, influenced by Greek and Judeo-Christian thought, religion has always played an essential role in the lives of Americans. In the United States the vast majority of those responding to public polls believe in God (Sakaki and Suzuki 1983; Warner 1993). Indeed, according to a Gallup poll, if a person has no religious beliefs, he or she will be subject to a negative image (Gallup 1990).

Traditional Chinese cultural values, especially family values, are much influenced by Confucianism, which is primarily concerned with harmony within human society (Bond 1991; Hsu 1981; Tu 1990). In the Confucian tradition, there is an emphasis that a human being exists in relationship to others. An individual is born into a family or a group and cannot prosper alone; the success of an individual depends on the harmony and strength of the group. At the core of the traditional Confucian value system is a set of behavioral principles enforcing vertical hierarchies of dominance. In this system, seniority and parental authority were greatly respected. Hence, obedience, unselfishness, responsibility, hard work, and thrift are highly emphasized in Confucian teaching for the purpose of cultivating oneself and honoring the family name (Ho 1994). Although these qualities are also part of the Protestant work ethic, this work ethic appears to have eroded recently (Chen 1992; Spence 1985).

Thus, the discussions of traditional American values and Chinese values depict the two countries as having very different cultural traditions. The theory of individualism and collectivism also generates complementary expectations. In cross-cultural studies, American culture is often considered an individualism-oriented culture, in contrast with Chinese culture, which emphasizes collectivism. Several scholars have elaborated the contrasting characteristics of individualism and collectivism. According to Hofstede (1980), individualism is a preference for a loosely knit social framework in which individuals are supposed to take care of themselves and their immediate families only. Collectivism is a preference for a tightly knit social framework in which individuals can expect their relatives, clan, or other in-group members to look after them in exchange for unquestioning loyalty. From a psychological perspective, Triandis (1995) suggested a similar distinction between collectivism and individualism. In collective cultures, individuals are willing to subordinate their personal goals to the goals of various in-groups, such as the family, the tribe, or the work group. By contrast, in individualistic cultures, it is considered acceptable for individuals to place personal goals ahead of the group's goals.

Empirical studies comparing children's scholastic achievement show that Chinese (as well as other Asian) children are consistently among the highest achievers in international mathematics and science competitions. To determine possible causes, Chen and Uttal (1988) have conducted a cross-national study of American and Chinese parents' beliefs about, and expectations for, their children's level of educational achievement. The results show that parents' expectations for, and satisfaction with, their children's academic performance differ greatly between the United States and China. Controlling for students' grades and test scores, Chinese parents are more likely than American parents to have higher expectations for their children's performance and express dissatisfaction with their children's test scores. Chen and Uttal infer that this is mainly due to the influence of traditional Chinese values concerning human malleability and human potentials. In traditional Chinese thinking, the level of achievement is considered to come more from diligent work and effort rather than from innate ability. This belief persists today.

In investigating cultural variations in childrearing practices among Chinese, immigrant Chinese, and Caucasian American parents, Lin and Fu (1990) analyzed the questionnaires completed by the mothers and fathers of 138 children from families in Taiwan and the United States. Their findings show that, compared with Caucasian American parents, parents of Chinese origin emphasize more achievement, parental control, and encouragement of independence for children. Both Chinese and immigrant Chinese parents tend to rate higher on these items than Caucasian American parents. While the higher ratings on achievement and parental control among parents of Chinese origin are consistent with the literature, the higher scores given by Chinese and Chinese American parents to independence seem to contradict traditional Chinese cultural values. The findings also suggest that parental control and a child's independence may not be contradictory in Chinese childrearing practices.

With regard to socialization values, researchers seem to agree that, traditionally, Chinese parents have been more concerned with children's submissiveness and obedience to parents than their Western counterparts, although more tolerance of children's independence has been observed in young and better-educated parents (Bond 1991; Ho 1989; Ho and Kang 1984).

If the content of socialization is based on the salient cultural values of the society, the preceding discussion then suggests the following expectations. Due to the influence of national cultures, Americans and Chinese emphasize different values in children. In particular, Americans are more likely than Chinese to desire values reflecting Judeo-Christian tradition and individualism such as independence, determination, and religious faith. Chinese, on the other hand, are expected to endorse, more than Americans, values emphasized in Confucian teachings and collectivism-oriented culture. These values are obedience, hard work, thrift/savings, unselfishness, and responsibility. I also hypothesize that child socialization values have different sources in the United States and China.

In this discussion, I have explored the structure of childrearing values of Americans and Chinese and the factors suggested in theories and past research that influence childrearing values. Unlike Kohn (1977) and others, I believe that childrearing values are multifaceted and are influenced by a number of structural and cultural/national cultural variables as well as social class. I argue that a comparison between the kinds of qualities that Americans and Chinese desire in children tests the overall applicability of the theories developed in country-specific studies. The findings also show us where and how the two cultures converge and diverge.

In the chapters that follow, I turn to an empirical exploration of these ideas. In Chapter 3, I first describe the data and discuss the measures of the dependent and independent variables. Then, I outline the strategies for my analyses. Starting in Chapter 4, I undertake an empirical assessment of the hypotheses developed in this chapter.

NOTE

1. In extending Kohn's model, the Wrights included both men and women in the analysis, because they believe that an understanding of the socialization process would be aided if parental values of both fathers and mothers are examined.

Chapter 3

Data, Measures of Variables, and Strategies of Data Analysis

DATA AND SAMPLES

The present research uses data from the World Values Survey (WVS). Designed mainly for making cross-national comparisons of values and norms in a wide range of areas, the WVS collected data in 43 countries and regions in the period 1990–1993. The principal investigator was the World Values Study Group (1994), with fieldwork supported by sources within the participating country in most cases. All responses came from face-to-face interviews, with samples consisting of all adults ages 18 and older.

Useful for my purposes, the WVS contains information on the kinds of qualities that adults desire in children—childrearing values. Two samples in the WVS, one from the United States and one from China, are used in this study. The U.S. sample is a national representative sample with interviews conducted by the Gallup Organization in 1990. The Chinese data come from a representative sample of the urban population. The China Statistical Information Center collected data in July–December 1990 (Inglehart 1994). There is clearly a difference in the sampling frame of the two samples. Although the Chinese urban population is, in a sense, analogous to the U.S. civic population (because it is highly urbanized), one must remain aware of this difference throughout the study. This sampling difference is also controlled in data analysis. My data analysis is designed for two levels of analysis of childrearing values: within-country analysis and between-country analysis. Within-country analysis focuses on the links between social structure and childrearing values within each country. Since rural population is a small proportion of the U.S. population (about 15%), within-country analysis does not differentiate urban respondents from rural respondents. Between-country analysis examines cross-national similarities as well as differences in value orientations. I make comparisons between American urban respondents and Chinese respondents whenever it is appropriate.

Due to the fact that the Chinese sample was drawn from an urban population, I do not assume that the Chinese respondents are representative of the entire Chinese population. I do believe, however, that my findings can be useful as indicators of the childrearing expectations of Chinese urban residents.

A list of 11 value items pertaining to childrearing values appeared in the survey: good manners, independence, hard work, feeling of responsibility, imagination, tolerance/respect for other people, thrift/saving money and things, determination/perseverance, religious faith, unselfishness, and obedience. In the World Values Survey, all interviewees were asked to choose up to 5 items from the 11 items as the most important qualities that a child should be encouraged to learn at home. The original wording of the question can be found in Appendix A.

These items have a number of limitations. First, not all of them are identical to the values examined in previous research. While items such as independence, responsibility, good manners, and obedience are related to the autonomy/conformity dimension of value preferences and have received considerable attention (Alwin 1986, 1989; Kohn 1977; Wright and Wright 1976; Xiao and Andes 1999), others have rarely been examined up to now. Thus, this study is an extension, rather than a replication, of previous research.

Second, the nature of the data analyzed here is different from that of previous research on childrearing values. Traditionally, respondents in surveys or interviews were asked to either rate or rank a set of items pertaining to the qualities that people desire in children. Respondents in the WVS, however, were instructed to choose only 5 items from a list of 11 as important qualities that a child should learn at home. Caution should be used when comparing the findings from this study with those of other studies.

Finally, these items reflect general attitudes rather than the standards for behavior adopted by a respondent in childrearing activities. There is a difference between a respondent's thinking that it is important for a child to have certain qualities and actually emphasizing those qualities in childrearing practice. The present study focuses only on people's general attitudes.

Despite the limitations, the 11 value items provide a rare opportunity to examine childrearing values in the 1990s, when great changes took place in both the American and Chinese families. Furthermore, the inclusion of value items such as unselfishness and tolerance has also made it possible to test the existence of an emphasis on care in value orientations and the proposed gender difference in this value dimension. Last, since the purpose of the present study is to extend, but not to replicate, previous research, these differences are not serious limitations.

The samples in this study consist of the American and Chinese respondents who gave valid answers to the value question in the interview; that is, only those who selected 1 to 5 items were included in the analysis. I consider the responses of 6 items or more invalid because they are not consistent with the interview instructions. Furthermore, when more than 5 items are selected, the prioritization of certain values over others is lost. If these responses are included in the data analysis, problems arise in computing a measure of relative importance of the different childrearing values for the entire data set. In fact, quite a number of American respondents did not make a choice between the value items at all; they selected 10 or all 11 items in their answers to the value question! I excluded these nondifferentiating respondents. There is a total of 254 nondifferentiating respondents in the U.S. sample and 6 nondifferentiating respondents in the Chinese sample. As a result of the restriction and excluding cases with missing values, there are 1,575 Americans and 992 Chinese in the analysis samples out of 1,839 Americans and 1,000 Chinese in the total samples.

Due to the number of nondifferentiating respondents in the U.S. sample, I conducted tests of sampling bias. Differentiating Americans and nondifferentiating Americans are compared on several sociodemographic variables. Respondents with missing values are excluded from the comparison. Table 3.1 shows the results of the comparisons. Overall, the two groups are very similar with regard to gender, age, and educational distribution; however, there are significant differences in social class distribution of the two groups. Differentiating respondents are more likely than nondifferentiating respondents to be employed in professional and nonmanual occupations. Nondifferentiating Americans, on the other hand, are more likely than differentiating Americans to be managers and manual workers. The difference between the two groups in social class locations is significant at the level of p < .01. Since the nondifferentiating respondents showed little value preference, excluding them did not affect the relationship between class and values in my study.

Detailed demographic characteristics of American and Chinese respondents in the analysis samples are presented in Table 3.2. Of the 1,575 American respondents, there are 50 percent men and 50 percent women. In the Chinese analysis sample, there are 60 percent men and 40 percent women. The majority of the American respondents (81.4%) classified themselves as white, 10.8 percent as black, 5.7 percent as Hispanic, and 2.1 percent as Asians or others. No ethnic distinction is

Table 3.1
Demographic Characteristics of Differentiating and Nondifferentiating Respondents in the U.S. Sample

	Differentiating		Nondifferentiating		
	n	(%)	n	(%)	Chi-square
Gender					
Male	772	(50.0)	126	(49.6)	0.02
Female	771	(50.0)	128	(50.4)	
Age					
18-24	154	(9.9)	20	(7.9)	2.56
25-44	631	(40.6)	107	(42.5)	
45-64	455	(29.2)	81	(32.1)	
65 or older	316	(20.3)	44	(17.5)	
Education					
Less than H.S.	344	(24.4)	63	(30.1)	3.27
H.S.	452	(32.0)	61	(29.2)	
More than H.S.	617	(43.7)	85	(40.7)	
Social Class					
Manager	144	(10.6)	37	(17.5)	15.78**
Professional	343	(25.2)	39	(18.5)	
Foremen	59	(4.3)	12	(5.7)	
Nonmanual	293	(21.6)	33	(15.6)	
Manual	520	(38.3)	90	(42.7)	

** p < .01

Table 3.2
Demographic Characteristics of the U.S. and Chinese Analysis Sample[a]

	United States		China	
	%	(n)	%	(n)
Gender				
Male	50.0	(772)	59.9	(593)
Female	50.0	(771)	40.1	(397)
Race[b]				
Caucasian	81.4	(1250)	--	--
African American	10.8	(166)	--	--
Hispanic American	5.7	(88)	--	--
Other[c]	2.1	(32)	--	--
Age				
18-24	9.9	(154)	16.2	(161)
25-44	40.6	(631)	44.4	(440)
45-64	29.2	(455)	35.9	(356)
65 or older	20.3	(316)	3.5	(35)
Mean (in years)	46.9		39.3	
Standard Deviation	17.7		14.0	
Education				
Less than H.S.	24.3	(344)	38.1	(341)
H.S.	32.0	(452)	27.1	(242)
More than H.S.	43.7	(617)	34.8	(311)
Parental Status				
Nonparent	23.6	(371)	22.3	(221)
Current Parent	44.8	(705)	71.7	(709)
Past Parent	31.7	(499)	6.0	(59)
Social Class				
Manager	12.6	(172)	15.2	(150)
Professional	24.5	(334)	10.0	(98)
Foremen	4.2	(58)	20.5	(202)
Nonmanual	21.0	(287)	19.4	(191)
Manual	37.7	(514)	34.9	(343)

a. Total sample size is 1,575 for the United States and 992 for China.
b. About 98 percent of Chinese respondents identified themselves as Han people or as ethnic Chinese first and then as ethnic minority members.
c. Asians and others

made for Chinese respondents because some ethnic minorities are indistinguishable in Chinese cities, and more than 98 percent of the respondents claim themselves as Han people (*Han Zu*) or ethnic Chinese.[1] In terms of age, the two samples show different patterns. At the young and middle age levels (18–24, 25–44, and 45–64), there are proportionally more Chinese than Americans. At the old-age level (65 or older), the trend is reversed; there are proportionally more Americans than Chinese, 18 percent versus 3 percent.

Differences in the education of the respondents between the two countries are also clearly observed. On the one hand, 24.3 percent of Americans versus 38.1 percent of Chinese did not graduate from high school. On the other hand, about 44 percent of Americans versus 35 percent of Chinese had an education beyond high school. Finally, the proportion of parents living with children in the Chinese sample is much higher than that in the U.S. sample, 72 percent versus 45 percent. This is due to two demographic features of the Chinese population: virtually universal marriage and childbearing and the relatively large number of extended households. Results from cross-tabulations show that, among the survey respondents aged 25 and older, Chinese in every single age group are much more likely than Americans to report having at least one child and to be living in households with a child or children. Thus, compared with Americans, Chinese tend to be younger, less-educated, and more likely to be parents living with children. Comparisons of the two samples by age and parental status are presented in Appendix B.

In the aspect of social class (I discuss the definition of social class in the next section of this chapter), the largest category is the manual workers for both countries. In the United States, for example, 41 percent of the respondents are located in the manual worker category. In China the figure is 35 percent. The second largest group in the United States is professional workers. More than 24 percent of the total respondents are found in this category. In China, however, only 10 percent of the respondents are identified as professionals. The second largest group of Chinese is foremen/supervisors. About 21 percent of Chinese interviewed are located in this category, whereas just a little over 4 percent of Americans are found in the same category. These differences in the percentage distributions of social class reflect economic development in the two societies. The United States is a postindustrial society, where the economy is based on information, financial industries, services, and production of goods. China is an industrializing country. Its economy is mainly based on production of goods.

Comparing the preceding information with the major demographic characteristics of the general population in the two countries, I can evaluate the representativeness of the U.S. and Chinese analysis samples. In the U.S. sample, there are 50 percent men, and 50 percent women. In the U.S. general population of persons 18 years or older, 41 percent are men, and 59 percent are women (U.S. Department of Commerce, Bureau of the Census 1990). In the Chinese analysis sample, there are 60 percent men and 40 percent women. In the Chinese general population of persons 18 years or older in urban areas, 52 percent are men, and 48 percent are women (China's Population Census Office and State Statistical Bureau 1993).[2] Thus, men are overrepresented in the samples from both countries.

With respect to race, a majority, 81.4 percent, of the American respondents are white. Black and Hispanic respondents account for 10.8 percent and 5.7 percent, respectively. The ethnic makeup of the general population, according to the U.S. census data, shows that whites are 81 percent, blacks are 12 percent, and Hispanics are 5 percent (U.S. Department of Commerce, Bureau of the Census 1990). This discrepancy is very slight; therefore, generalization of the results is justified.

The mean age of the U.S. sample is 47 years, while the mean age of all adults over the age of 18 in the U.S. general population is 41. In this sense, the U.S. sample is biased toward those who are older. Within the Chinese sample, the mean age is 39 years. The mean age of the general population 18 years of age or older in urban China is 38.[3] Thus, the Chinese sample is representative of urban population with respect to age.

The two countries differ not only in major demographic characteristics but also in cultural/historical traditions and social/economic systems. To investigate the relationships between childrearing values and their predictors within each country as well as the national cultural boundaries of those relationships, I need to construct not only generic explanatory factors but also measures of relevant, culturally specific variables. I now describe more precisely the variables that I use to examine the hypotheses and discuss how these measures differ between the U.S. and Chinese samples.

SOCIAL CLASS VERSUS SOCIAL STATUS

Scholars of social stratification do not have consensus on the proper way to index people's different positions in the social structure. There is wide disagreement on how people differ in terms of power, prestige, and resources and how these differences in social positions affect other aspects of social and family life, including childrearing values. One conceptual difficulty is caused by differences between Marxist theory of class and Weberian concept of status. To Marx, capitalist society could be divided into two groups, the bourgeoisie and the proletariat, depending on the individual's relation to the means of production (Marx [1894] 1977). Weber, however, classified people based on their career opportunities and mobility patterns (Weber 1946).

Both Marxist and Weberian notions of social class have been expanded. To many social scientists, class and status are alternative conceptualizations of social structure. However, a key difference between the two theoretical concepts exists in contemporary stratification theories. While class theories group people into discrete categories in terms of their relationship to ownership, control of the means of production, and control over the labor power of others (Dahrendorf 1959; Wright 1976, 1985), status theories emphasize the hierarchical ordering of society as indexed by formal education, occupational status, and job income (Blau and Duncan 1967; Giddens 1973). Although much empirical work has focused on the gradations of social class and the dynamics of social mobility in the United States as well as other advanced industrial societies, the measure of categorical class remains an important concept in stratification research. Marxist class theorists argue that there are rigid boundaries between classes in terms of property, authority/control, and skill (Baxter 1994; Gagliani 1981; Lachmann 1990; Lockwood 1992). When people are asked about the society in which they live and where they locate themselves, they describe a class structure of different distinguishable segments and situate themselves in one of these segments. In research on capitalist Australia and postcommunist Hungary, Evans et al. (1992) report that individuals describe the past and the present in terms of class divisions.

Much of the past research on the class–parental values relationship employed the concept of socioeconomic status—a composite of occupation, education, and job income—but the categorical measure of class is also found to be a useful concept in interpreting value differences. In a study on job experiences, self-esteem, and fathering, Grimm-Thomas and Perry-Jenkins (1994) used occupations and job conditions to define working class. In examining the psychological effect of social class in the United States, Japan, and Poland, Kohn et al. (1990) defined class in terms of ownership, control of the means of production, and control over the labor power of others for the three countries. They believe that the reason that social class affects parental values of self-direction versus conformity is that class position is determinative of how much control one has over the conditions of one's own work.

The United States and China are highly stratified societies. In both societies occupation is essential in locating individuals' positions in the social structure. The two countries, however, have distinctive cultures and political economic systems. While the United States is a Western, industrialized capitalist society, China is an Eastern, industrializing socialist society. Considering that the contemporary class structure in each nation is shaped by different history, culture, and political and economic systems, I constructed two class schemes, one for the United States and one for China. Due to the differences, the two class schemes are somewhat different in definitions and categories but broadly comparable in conceptualization.

MEASURING SOCIAL CLASS IN THE UNITED STATES

Class location in the United States is conceptualized and defined by borrowing Wright's (1985) model, which distinguishes class locations on the basis of possession and control of property assets, organizational assets, and skill assets, and by following Gagliani's (1985) argument, which distinguishes nonmanual workers from manual workers on the basis of employment conditions. During the last two decades, many changes in the nature of work have occurred because of technological advances in computers and telecommunications (Crouter and Manke 1994). These advances have blurred the line between manual and nonmanual work, but they have not fundamentally changed occupational conditions of manual and nonmanual workers. As Kohn et al. (1990, p. 970) argued, "The basic situation of nonmanual workers—in terms of job security, employment in an office or commercial setting, payment in the form of salary rather than hourly or piecework wages, and fringe benefits . . . is distinctly more akin to that of management."

Five social classes are defined in the U.S. sample:

1. Employers and managers are defined by their possession and/or control of property assets, organizational assets, and/or the labor power of others. The self-employed are included in this category.
2. Professional workers are defined as those who possess only skill assets.

3. Foremen and supervisors are distinguished from managers because the former have no real control over the property assets and organizational assets and only very limited control over the labor power of others.
4. Nonmanual workers are nonsupervisory employees whose work is predominantly white-collar and nonmanual in character.
5. Manual workers are nonsupervisory employees whose work is predominantly blue-collar and manual in character.

MEASURING SOCIAL CLASS IN CHINA

To conceptualize and index social class in China, it is important to take account not only of those general considerations that apply to any state socialist society but also of the cultural history of China. Thus, the following considerations are taken in constructing a social class index for China.

First, ownership of the means of production, the basic category of Marx's theory of social class, was not a class criterion in China until the 1980s, when the market economy emerged. This is not to say that before the 1980s there were no individuals in China who were self-employed, but the number was very small (Li 1994). During the three decades of 1949 to 1979, self-employment and private business were discouraged and sometimes forbidden in China, especially in urban areas. Private ownership of business was considered a product of capitalism and thus often criticized. As a social group, the self-employed in urban China were mainly made up of people who could not find employment in state- or collective-owned enterprises (Li 1994). Furthermore, compared to petty bourgeoisie in capitalist societies, the self-employed and small-business owners in China had very limited independence in planning and organizing their work before the economic reform took place.

After the economic reform, running a private and independent business or enterprise was permitted and even encouraged by the government. By the early 1980s, most state- and collective-owned enterprises were overstaffed. Many work units could pay their employees only 50 percent to 75 percent of their full wages/salaries. To avoid layoff and solve the problem of redundant personnel, many work units implemented the "leave without pay" policy. Under this policy, employees were encouraged to take long-term leave to run their own business. If they were not successful in their private business, they could return to their positions in the work units. This policy stimulated the development of private business. Many workers, professionals, and cadres took a leave to start their own business. As a result, there was a rapid increase in the number of self-employed in China during the late 1980s and early 1990s. Many laid-off workers were also forced to work out of their homes to make a living. In my Chinese sample, close to 23 percent of the Chinese respondents claimed themselves as self-employed. In the total population, however, the self-employed constituted less than 3 percent of all employed Chinese in 1992 (China Daily 1994).

It should also be noted that the self-employed and owners of private business are considered synonymous in China. Anyone who makes earnings and is not employed by others is said to be self-employed, regardless if he or she is a multimillionaire businessperson or a street peddler. At the same time, due to the relatively low social prestige and the maltreatment of businesspeople during the 1949–1979 period, some owners of private business are cautious about their social identity, especially in public surveys. They prefer to identify themselves as managers or cadres (Li 1994). Thus, it is very hard in China to operationalize in a meaningful way the concepts of petty bourgeoisie/self-employed and owners of private business.

Second, as in other state socialist societies, stratification in China is organized around the state socialist redistributive economy rather than a market economy. Resource transfers and the location of individuals in the social structure are largely determined by political power rather than by market mechanisms. Thus, the crucial criteria in social class identification are control of property assets, organizational assets, and labor, possession of skills, and division between manual and nonmanual work (Wright 1985).

Finally, in China, classes and occupations are historically and culturally synonymous. The four widely known classes—gentry, peasants, workers, and merchants—in traditional Chinese society are, in fact, occupational classifications. These four social classes were so stable that they lasted nearly 2,000 years until the early years of the twentieth century. Due to the social, political, and economic changes in modern China, this occupational structure has altered, but the association between occupation and class location has not changed. Recent research on social stratification in China has empirically identified occupations as the major determinant of class location (Li 1994; Peng 1992; Walder 1995). In my analysis, the class locations of Chinese respondents are determined by their occupations. The self-employed are also classified according to their occupation titles.

A total of five social classes are defined in the Chinese sample:

1. Administrative cadres and managers are defined as employees in major decision-making positions.
2. Professional workers are defined as those who possess only skill assets (teachers, accountants, lawyer, sciences and technology workers).
3. Supervisors and foremen include administrative personnel and employees who have limited supervisory authority.
4. Nonmanual workers are nonsupervisory employees whose work is predominantly white-collar and nonmanual in character.
5. Manual workers are nonsupervisory employees whose work is predominantly blue-collar and manual in character.

In both countries, respondents who were not employed at the time of the survey were classified according to their last occupation. Those who never had a paid job or were members of the armed forces were not included.[4] Farmers and agricultural workers in the U.S. sample were also excluded to increase its comparability to the Chinese sample.[5] Each of the five class locations in the two countries is coded dichotomously (1 = yes, and 0 = no).[6]

MEASURES OF OTHER INDEPENDENT VARIABLES

Gender

This variable simply distinguishes women from men. It is coded 1 = female, and 0 = male.

Education

Previous research indicates that the valuation of children's autonomy or conformity is partially a function of one's education. In the WVS, however, information on respondents' education is not adequate to allow for a straightforward measure of the variable. Regarding education, interviewees were asked only to state the age at which they completed formal education. Ten categories were provided; they range from 1 = 12 years of age or earlier to 10 = 21 years of age or older. To measure education, I used the best approximation that I could. Specifically, the variable is recoded for each country as 1 = less than high school (if a respondent completed formal education at or before the age of 17), 2 = high school (if completed education at 18 or 19 years of age), and 3 = more than high school (if completed education at 20 years of age or older). Because both the United States and China have a public education policy and because children (of urban families in China) start schooling uniformly at 6 or 7 years of age, I believe this measure is relatively accurate.

Age

This variable is measured in years. Each respondent in the WVS was asked to state his or her date of birth. The interviewer then verified the exact age of the respondent.

People's age may be related to conformity valuation primarily because age is indicative of a cohort effect. Alwin (1984, 1988, 1990) has shown that at the aggregate level the conformity orientation toward children in the United States has declined over time, and the proportion of the population valuing autonomy has increased over time. Parents raised during a period when the culture more strongly emphasized obedience in children (e.g., the 1940s and 1950s) may bear a legacy of that socialization experience in valuing more conformity for children. These would more likely be older parents. Parents raised in the later period (e.g., the 1960s and 1970s) would be more likely to stress autonomy for children, because they may have been exposed to socialization values favoring autonomy. These would more likely be younger parents.

Age Cohort

To further understand the effects of age cohort, an age cohort variable is created to assess the influence of political movements on people's socialization ideals for children. Four age groups are distinguished. Group 1 includes those who were 18–24 years old at the time of the survey. Group 2 contains respondents who were 25–44 years old. Group 3 is made up 45–64 year-old respondents. Group 4 includes those who were 65 or older at the time of the survey. Given the nature and the frequency of political events that occurred in modern and contemporary China, I expect the age group variable to be especially meaningful in the analysis of the Chinese sample. The respondents in group 1 (18–24 years old) grew up mainly in the era of the economic reform and were not parents yet. Most of the Chinese in group 2 (25–44 years old) were parents of a single child. The respondents in group 3 (45–64 years old) had experienced the Cultural Revolution as adults.

Group 4 (65 and older) respondents mainly grew up in the prerevolution era and experienced all the important political events in the People's Republic of China.

Race

For the U.S. data, race is measured by two dummy variables distinguishing African Americans and Hispanics from Caucasians and others. Since there was no oversampling of racial or ethnic minorities in the U.S. sample of 1990, it is not statistically sound to make other distinctions in data analysis. Two entries in the WVS are relevant to the identification of race. The first was a self-identification. Each interviewee in the American sample was asked to identify himself or herself as one of the following: (1) Hispanic American; (2) Black American; (3) white American; (4) Asian American; and (5) American first and a member of some ethnic group second. The second entry was an identification made by the interviewer. In self-identification, about 30 percent of the respondents selected the "I am an American first" category. I classified these respondents into racial/ethnic groups according to the interviewer's observations. Thus, each of the two race variables (African Americans and Hispanic Americans) is a combination of self-identification and interviewer's observation.

In the Chinese sample, more than 98 percent of the respondents identified themselves as Chinese or ethnic Chinese first. Since ethnic minorities are small in numbers in urban population and indistinguishable from the majority, no ethnic distinction could be made.

In addition to the preceding sociodemographic characteristics, the following independent variables are incorporated in the data analysis in order to assess the overall relationships between childrearing values and their predictors in the United States and China.

Parental Status

Ordinarily, measuring parental status should not be a difficult task if the data provide information on the variable. Unfortunately, there is no unambiguous designation of parental status of respondents in the WVS. I therefore infer parental status from information about whether respondents ever had any children and whether they were living in a household with one or more children at the time of the interview. In my analysis, parental status has three categories: current parents, past parents, and nonparents. Current parents are respondents who reported having at least one child and living in a household with one or more children at the time of the interview. Past parents are those who have had at least one child but were not living in a household with any children. Nonparents are those who never had any children and were living in a household without a child.

It should be noted that not all current parents live in nuclear families. The vast majority of them are parents with minor/dependent children in nuclear families. But some of them may be grandparents living with grown children in extended families. Since grandparents in extended families do play more active childrearing roles, I do not consider this a serious problem. Each of the three categories is coded dichotomously, and the nonparent is the excluded category in multiple regression analyses.

Family Size

Two variables are used to measure the family size: the number of children ever had and the number of children living at home. They are coded as 0 = no child, 1 = 1 child, 2 = 2 children, 3 = 3 children, 4 = 4 children, 5 = 5 children, and 6 = 6 children or more.

Occupational Autonomy

A key argument in Kohn's class–value theory is that job characteristics associated with social class explain a large part of the variations in childrearing values. One of such characteristics is the discretionary content or autonomy of the job. This refers to the amount of discretion that the person has in a job role. My measure of job autonomy is based on a respondent's self-report on how much decision-making freedom he or she has or had on the job. The response is coded so that a high score on the variable indicates more freedom. The scores of this continuous variable range from 1 (representing least job freedom) to 10 (indicating most job freedom).

Attitude toward Women's Labor Force Participation

Many feminist and family scholars agree that attitudes toward women's roles in the family are critical to understanding women's and men's values and beliefs. The WVS includes a series of questions on people's orientations toward the roles and status of women. Drawing on seven questions on respondents' attitudes toward labor force participation versus full-time engagement in domestic roles as a source of meaning in a woman's life, I constructed a measure of the attitudes toward women's domestic roles by summing the responses to each of the questions. The possible responses to the first six questions are "4 = strongly agree," "3 = agree," "2 = disagree," and "1 = strongly disagree." These questions are:

1. A working mother can establish just as warm and secure a relationship with her children as a mother who does not work (V218).
2. A preschool child is likely to suffer if his or her mother works (V219).
3. A job is all right, but what most women really want is a home and children (V220).
4. Being a housewife is just as fulfilling as working for pay (V221).
5. Having a job is the best way for a woman to be an independent person (V222).
6. Both the husband and wife should contribute to household income (V223).

Question 7 asks the respondents whether they "4 = strongly approve," "3 = somewhat approve," "2 = somewhat disapprove," or "1 = strongly disapprove" of the women's movement (V294). Questions 2–4 (V219, V220, and V221) are reverse-coded: the more that a respondent disagrees with them, the higher the score on the scale. The other four questions in the scale are coded so that the more a respondent agrees with or approves of them, the higher the score. The responses to each of the seven questions were summed to obtain a total scale score. The measure ranges from 7 to 28, where low scores indicate an emphasis on women's homemaker roles and high scores indicate a valuation of women's labor force participation. The Cronbach's alpha coefficient for this scale is .60 for the American respondents, but it is .23 for the Chinese respondents. One possible explanation for the low alpha for the China data may be that these questions are not very meaningful to Chinese respondents. Since 1949, full-time homemaking has rarely been an option for adult Chinese women, especially in urban areas. Due to necessity, urban Chinese women are expected to combine full-time work with motherhood. In an effort to identify a subset of the items that may be meaningful to Chinese respondents, I ran a factor analysis of the 7 items, but the results are unsatisfactory. I therefore use the scale in analyzing the U.S. data only.

Sense of Control

Question 95 in the WVS asks all respondents to use a 10-point scale to indicate how much freedom or choice and control they feel that they have in their lives. While a point of 10 indicates maximum freedom and choice, a point of 1 represents minimum freedom or choice.

Religiosity

The religiosity variable enables me to tap the effect of religious involvement on child socialization ideals. Religiosity is measured by two indicators included in all interviews: importance of God and religious attendance. Importance of God is measured by the question: "How important is God in your life?" The responses range from 1 (not at all) to 10 (very). Religious attendance is measured by the question: "Apart from weddings, funerals and christenings, about how often do you attend religious services these days?" The responses are 1= never, 2= less often, 3= once a year, 4= other specific holidays, 5= Christmas/Easter Day, 6= once a month, 7= once a week, and 8= more than once a week.[7] The responses for these two questions were added to form a single measure of religiosity (coefficient alpha equals .86).

Although Confucianism, Taoism, and Buddhism are often considered three major religions in China, they are not formal religions in Western terms. First of all, none of the three belief systems involve church service or attendance. Furthermore, none of them have a place for God. Thus, the measure of religiosity that I described is used only in the analysis of the U.S. sample. There are certainly alternative methods to measure "religiosity" in China. Unfortunately, the WVS does not contain the relevant information for me to do so.

Conventionality

Conventional individuals are those who value filial piety, identified by an affirmative response to the question of "regardless of what the qualities and faults of one's parents are, one must always love and respect them."

Urban Location

This variable differentiates between urban and rural respondents in the U.S. sample. Since the Chinese sample was drawn from the urban population, the variable is created mainly for the purpose of making comparisons between urban American respondents and Chinese respondents.

Due to national differences in the characteristics that distinguish urban from rural areas, the distinction between urban and rural population varies by country (Shryock et al. 1992). Although the Chinese sample contains only the urban residents, information on city size is incomplete in the WVS; about one-third of the respondents are missing values on the question. Thus, it is impossible to create an American urban sample that is comparable with the Chinese sample. Guided by the U.S. census definition of urban population, I identify the urban respondents in the U.S. sample as those who live in an area of 2,000 people or more.[8]

National Culture

By national culture, I refer to a system of basic common values that help shape the behavior of the people in a given society. Because there are no perfect measures of national culture in the survey, I use nation as a surrogate of culture. The nation variable distinguishes Chinese respondents from Americans respondents in the United States–China comparisons.

DEPENDENT VARIABLES

To achieve parsimony and simplify the interrelationship among a set of value items, measures of childrearing values are usually constructed through a factor analysis of a list of items that people are asked to rate or rank as most/least desirable/important traits for children to have. Kohn (1977) and others (e.g., Spade 1991) have demonstrated that childrearing values mainly form one value dimension on which autonomy and conformity constitute the two poles.[9]

For the purpose of examining the internal structure of the 11 value items and data reduction, I also performed an exploratory factor analysis, separately for the U.S. sample and the Chinese sample. Factor analyses of the American sample suggest that a two-factor solution was appropriate for the data. Table 3.3 presents the factor patterns and loadings from the two factors generated from the factor analysis of the 11 value items in the U.S. data.

As observed in Table 3.3, the factor loadings suggest that two distinct substantive factors underlie the data. Factor 1 represents valuation of autonomy versus conformity in children. It is marked by key items that are representative of valuation of autonomy and conformity, and these items have high loadings (both positive and negative) on the factor. The items indicating autonomy have large positive loadings. These items are "independence" (r = .592), "determination" (r = .558), and "imagination" (r = .479). The items representing conformity have high

Table 3.3
Factor Patterns and Loadings for the U.S. Data

Value items	Factor 1[a]	Factor 2[b]
Obedience	−0.568	0.306
Good Manners	−0.506	−0.183
Religious Faith	−0.488	−0.011
Independence	0.592	−0.128
Determination	0.558	0.295
Imagination	0.479	−0.062
Unselfishness	−0.075	0.603
Tolerance/Respect	0.066	0.446
Hard Work	0.040	−0.579
Thrift/Saving	−0.244	−0.422
Responsibility	0.184	−0.257
Eigenvalues	1.813	1.377

a. Italicized negative values make up the conformity value dimension. Italicized positive values make up the autonomy value dimension.

b. Italicized positive values make up the care orientation.

Table 3.4
Factor Patterns and Loadings for the Chinese Data

Value items	Factor 1[a]	Factor 2[b]
Obedience	0.534	−0.175
Hard Work	0.518	−0.220
Thrift/Saving	0.663	0.068
Independence	−0.366	−0.174
Determination	−0.631	−0.115
Imagination	−0.376	−0.295
Good Manners	0.108	−0.660
Unselfishness	−0.115	0.452
Tolerance/Respect	0.055	0.666
Responsibility	0.194	0.317
Religious Faith	−0.007	0.127
Eigenvalues	1.730	1.413

a. Italicized positive values make up the conformity value dimension. Italicized negative values make up the autonomy value dimension.

b. Italicized positive values make up the care orientation.

negative factor loadings. They are "obedience" ($r = -.568$), "good manners" ($r = -.506$), and "religious faith" ($r = -.488$).

Loadings of the value items on factor 2 indicate that it is also a bipolar dimension. The bipolar dimension is between "unselfishness" ($r = .603$) and "tolerance/respect" ($r = .446$), on the one hand, and "hard work" ($r = -.579$) and "thrift/saving" ($r = -.422$), on the other. This dimension could be viewed to roughly indicate the valuation of careorientation (or other-directed orientation) versus emphasis on achievement/work ethic values of the respondents. The item "responsibility" does not attain satisfactory loading on either of the two factors.

Factor extraction results from the Chinese data are summarized in Table 3.4. A varimax rotation was performed to obtain the factor structure presented here. The 11 value items also clustered mainly on two factors. The first factor represents a value dimension of autonomy versus conformity. The autonomy pole is made up of 3 items that have high negative loadings on the factor.[10] These items are "independence"(r = −.366), "determination" (r = −.631), and "imagination" (r = −.367). The conformity pole is defined by the clustering of items that have high positive loadings on the factor. They are "obedience" (r = .534), "hard work" (r = .518), and "thrift/saving" (r = .663).

The second factor is also marked by two kinds of value items. On the one end, "unselfishness" (r = .452), "tolerance/respect" (r = .666), and "responsibility" (r = .317) registered large positive loadings on the factor. On the other end, "good manners" (r = −.660) attained large negative loading. While the meanings of the care orientation is relatively straightforward, the interpretation of the single item pole of "good manners" is less clear. The item "religious faith" did not load well on either of the factors.

Comparing these results from the two countries, it is clear that there are similarities as well as differences in the structure and clustering patterns of the value items. The number of similarities is impressive. First, in both the United States and China, the exploratory factor analyses of the 11 value items extracted two factors. Second, both factors are bipolar-dimensional in each country, though the interpretation of the second Chinese factor is not a simple one. Finally and most importantly, the structure and meanings of the factors are essentially comparable between the United States and China. The differences, however, should not be overlooked. Among them the most important one is that the items made up of each factor are somewhat different for the United States and China. Caution should be used when making comparisons between the two countries.

To summarize, the results show that these 11 value items do not measure just one value dimension for the U.S. or China data; rather, they suggest the presence of two basic themes for parental valuation in each country. Both themes have a bipolar dimension. The first theme is the valuation of autonomy versus conformity in children. In both the United States and China, factor 1 represents the first theme. It is defined by key items of "independence" and "obedience," with different additional items loading in each country to "color" the dimension a little differently. In terms of the autonomy pole, the additional two items are identical—"determination" and "imagination." This suggests that the items indicative of a valuation of autonomy in children have semantic equivalence across the United States and China. In other words, these items carry the same socially understood meanings in each culture. The clustering of the items made up of the conformity pole presents a different picture, however. The two clusters do not share similar items except for "obedience." However, the large negative loadings of "good manners" and "religious faith" on the factor for the United States and "hard work" and "thrift/saving" for China indicate that these items have functional equivalence in measuring conformity in each culture. They represent culture-specific forms of conformity.

Factor 2 represents the second theme, an essentially bipolar dimension between the valuation of a care orientation versus achievement/work ethic values for the United States and a prioritization of care-oriented values over good manners for China. While factor 2 represents an interesting value dimension in each country, only the emphasis on care-oriented values is relevant for the present study.

For the purpose of testing the theoretical hypotheses discussed in Chapter 2 and for the ease of making cross-cultural comparisons, three dependent variables are constructed within each country. The first dependent variable is the valuation of autonomy in children. It is created by summing the scores for each respondent based on his or her responses to the value items making up the autonomy value dimension. These value items are "independence," "imagination," and "determination." Since each of the 11 value items is a dummy variable coded as 1 = selected, and 0 = not, the scores of the autonomy variable range from 0 to 3. On this scale, high scores indicate an emphasis on autonomy values. The second dependent variable, a valuation of conformity, is measured by a scale summing the scores of the values making up the conformity dimension in childrearing values within each country. For the United States, the variable is a summary score of "obedience," "good manners," and "religious faith." For China the variable is a summary score of "obedience," "hard work," and "thrift/saving." The scores also range from 0 to 3, where high scores represent a valuation of conformity. The third dependent variable is the valuation of a care orientation in children. It is assessed by summing the responses to the two items clearly representing a care orientation—"tolerance/respect" and "unselfishness." Again, high scores indicate a stronger emphasis on care-oriented values in children. Hence, while the valuation of autonomy and the care orientation scale are identical in the United States and China, the valuation of conformity is culturally specific.

Another option to measure the dependent variables is to use the factor scores computed in the factor analysis. This would yield two variables, the valuation of autonomy versus conformity and the valuation of a care orientation. The first variable would have to be seen to represent one value dimension with two poles opposite to each other. That is, a greater valuation of autonomy means less valuation of conformity. The percentage distributions of the item selections indicate otherwise, however (results not shown here). For example, American women are significantly more likely than American men to select both "independence" and "religious faith," even though the two value items belong to the two opposite poles of the autonomy/conformity dimension of the childrearing values. In the factor analysis, the selection of "independence" receives a positive (+) loading and "religious faith" a negative (−) loading (see Table 3.3). Since the final factor score for the variable (the valuation of autonomy versus conformity) results from adding the factor score coefficients of the six items representing the factor, the real difference in value selections can become obscured. In the summary factor score, the positive and negative scores balance out each other.[11]

The additive scales that I choose to use enable me to treat autonomy and conformity as two separate value domains, not necessarily opposite to each other. Given the method of data collection in the WVS, I believe that measuring the childrearing values with the additive scales is more appropriate than the traditional factor score measures. Previous research on childrearing values all imposed some kind of value-rating or value-ranking requirement on respondents. The underlying premise of the measures of the ratings and rankings is that childrearing values are inherently competitive. It is assumed that values such as autonomy and conformity are contrasting to each other. Respondents are forced to make choices between them.

Can people value both autonomy and conformity in children at the same time? Results based on the percentage distributions of the values in the WVS suggest that autonomy and conformity may not be the two opposite ends of a single value as typically believed. Autonomy and conformity may be separate and distinct values, with distinct, rather than antonymous, meanings. In the exploratory factor analysis of the U.S. data, the first factor is often seen as a single value dimension, with autonomy and conformity representing two poles. In this value dimension, three items make up the autonomy pole and three items make up the conformity pole. I believe that items representing the two poles can be valued equally. Behaviorally, parents can certainly attempt to develop the two kinds of qualities in their children. I can find no logical or necessary polarity between these qualities or any logical reason that parents necessarily must, in their everyday lives, make choice between these traits in rearing their children. Whether or not one quality is valued more than the other in the everyday context may vary with the situation.

In this sense, it is valid to treat autonomy and conformity as two separate and distinct values. The method also makes the interpretation of the regression coefficients in the multiple regression analyses more intuitive.

NOTES

1. China is a multiethnic nation with 92 percent Han people and 8 percent ethnic minority groups. The largest ethnic minority groups are Chuang, Hui, Uyghur, Yi, and Miao. However, the residency of the ethnic minorities is not evenly spread in China. Most of them live in minority autonomous regions.

2. I did the calculation based on data from China's Population Census Office and State Statistical Bureau (1993, Table 4.5, pp. 18-21).

3. Ibid.

4. A total of 59 respondents (53 female and 6 male) reported that they never had a job.

5. The Residence Registration System (*Hukou*) in China does not allow people engaged in agricultural work to live in the city. Thus, the Chinese sample does not have farmers or agricultural workers.

6. Since the self-employed are often considered to share the same class location with the employers and managers in Western societies and since the truly self-employed in China cannot be unambiguously identified in the Chinese data, they are not given a separate class location here.

7. The answers to the question were originally coded as 1 = More than once a week, 2 = Once a week, 3 = Once a month, 4 = Christmas/Easter Day, 5 = Other specific holidays, 6 = Once a year, 7 = Less often, and 8 = Never, practically never. For the purpose of constructing a religiosity scale, I reversed the original codings.

8. The U.S. census defines an urban area as a place with 2,500 inhabitants or more. In the WVS, however, size of town is not coded according to this definition. Instead, the following codes are used to measure the size of community: under 2,000; 2,000–5,000; 5,000–10,000; 10,000–20,000; 20,000–50,000; 50,000–100,000; 100,000–500,000; and 500,000 and more. Therefore, I

define the urban respondents in the U.S. sample as those who live in an area of 2,000 people or more.

9. Kohn's factoring procedures generated two factors. While he considered factor 1 indicative of self-direction versus conformity dimension, factor 2 was labeled a maturity dimension. This second factor/dimension was, however, treated very lightly in the book. The primary focus was on the self-direction versus conformity dimension.

10. After a varimax rotation, the items reflective of autonomy valuation (independence, determination, and imagination) received negative loadings on the factor, and the items indicative of conformity (obedience, hard work, and thrift/saving) obtained positive loadings. For the ease of making comparisons between the two societies, especially comparing the results in the regression analyses to follow in the later chapters, I reversed the direction/sign of the item loadings on the factor, giving autonomy values positive loadings and conformity values negative loadings. This simple change does not affect the latent structure of the factor or alter the nature of the relationship between the value items.

11. Using the factor loadings in Table 3.3, the scores for factor 1 (the valuation of autonomy versus conformity) can be obtained as:

factor 1 = $0.592 \times$ independence + $0.558 \times$ determination + $0.479 \times$ imagination $- 0.568 \times$ obedience $- 0.506 \times$ good manners $- 0.488 \times$ religious faith.

Chapter 4

Childrearing Values and Their Predictors: Findings from the U.S. Sample

In Chapter 2, I developed hypotheses about the effects of social class, gender, and several other relevant variables on the valuation of autonomy, conformity, and care orientation in children. The purpose of this chapter is to empirically test the hypotheses for the U.S. sample. There are six sections in the chapter. First I present overall class and gender differences in three childrearing values: the valuation of autonomy, conformity, and a care orientation in children. Then I clarify the effects of occupational autonomy on childrearing values. Next I explore the links between belief systems and value orientations. In the next section, I examine the roles of several other relevant variables on the childrearing orientations. The effects of family structural conditions and mothering on values are the focus of the following section. Finally I present multiple regression analyses and discuss the findings.

SOCIAL CLASS, GENDER, AND CHILDREARING VALUES

Do people of different social classes espouse different socialization values in children? To answer this question, I first examined the mean scores of the three values by class. Table 4.1 presents mean scores on the valuation of autonomy, conformity, and care orientation by social class. The results are mixed. In terms of the valuation of autonomy, professionals have the highest mean score, and manual workers have the lowest mean score. The mean score of owners/managers on autonomy valuation is the same as that of foremen/supervisors and very close to that of nonmanual workers. Thus, while the greater desire for this value by professionals and the less emphasis on the value by manual workers are consistent with previous findings, the non-difference displayed by owners/managers, foremen/supervisors, and nonmanual workers is unexpected. After all, owners and managers are more advantageously located in the social structure than the other two groups. Regarding the valuation of conformity, manual workers show the highest mean, while professional workers show the lowest mean. Here again, owners/managers, foremen/supervisors and nonmanual workers register similar mean scores on the variable. This suggests that although there is a class basis to the valuation of conformity, class location appears to make little difference to some people.

Looking over the valuation of care orientation, there is no significant difference among the five groups except for the professionals, who show

Table 4.1
Mean Scores and Standard Deviations of Childrearing Values by Social Class: U.S. Sample

Values	Social Class[a]					
	Owner/ Manager	Profes- sional	Foreman/ Supervisor	Non- Manual	Manual	F Value
Autonomy[b]	1.07	1.20	1.07	1.04	.79	13.79***
	(.95)	(.86)	(.87)	(.85)	(.75)	
Conformity[c]	1.49	1.33	1.53	1.51	1.71	10.56***
	(.86)	(.86)	(.88)	(.79)	(.85)	
Care Orientation[d]	.95	1.09	1.03	1.01	.94	2.88*
	(.63)	.65)	(.65)	(.65)	(.66)	
Number of Cases	172	334	58	287	514	

Note: Standard deviations are in parentheses.

a. Degree of freedom is 4; N = 1,365.
b. Scores range from 0 to 3; grand mean is .99.
c. Scores range from 0 to 3; grand mean is 1.54.
d. Scores range from 0 to 2; grant mean is 1.00.

* $p < .05$; *** $p < .001$

Table 4.2
Mean Scores and Standard Deviations of Childrearing Values by Gender:
U.S. Sample

Childrearing Values	Gender		
	Men	Women	T Value
Autonomy[a]	0.92	1.04	−2.73**
	(.85)	(.83)	
Conformity[b]	1.54	1.58	−0.85
	(.87)	(.84)	
Care Orientation[c]	0.97	1.02	−1.61
	(.66)	(.64)	
Number of Cases	772	771	

Note: Standard deviations are in parentheses.

a. Scores range from 0 to 3; grand mean is 0.98.
b. Scores range from 0 to 3; grand mean is 1.56.
c. Scores range from 0 to 2; grand mean is 0.99.

** $p < .01$

a greater emphasis on the care-oriented values in children. Overall, the mean scores of conformity are higher than the mean scores of autonomy for all social class locations. This is not surprising because results of previous investigations were mixed.

Previous research also suggests that men and women differ in their life experiences and value orientations. Drawing upon the literature, I hypothesized that there is a gender gap in the valuation of autonomy and care orientation and that women attach a greater importance than men to autonomy and care-orientated values. Table 4.2 presents mean scores and standard deviations on the three childrearing value scales by gender. As expected, women are, indeed, more likely than men to value autonomy (1.04 vs. 0.92, $p < .01$). However, the gender difference in the valuation of care orientation (women's $\overline{X} = 1.02$, men's $\overline{X} = 0.97$) is not statistically significant. There is no gender gap on the conformity measure either; women and men show similar desire for conformity in children (1.54 vs. 1.58).

To assess the overall relationship among the class, gender, and childrearing values, scores on the three value scales are subjected to a 5 (class) x 2 (gender) multivariate analysis of variance (MANOVA). Because members of different class groups differ in education, the MANOVA model controls for the effect of education. The results summarized in Table 4.3 confirm the findings discussed earlier. Significant effects of social class are found on all three value scales. Gender, on the other hand, is significantly related only to autonomy. It does not affect the valuation of conformity and a care orientation. The interaction effect between class and gender is significant for conformity but just misses attaining statistical significance for autonomy. However, the more striking finding is that the effect of education is substantially stronger than that of both social class and gender, suggesting that years of schooling is a more important source of value orientations. I take up this point later.

The analysis of variance, of course, does not show in what way social class and gender interact on childrearing values. With the findings from the MANOVA, my next question is, how do class and gender interact on the three value scales?

Table 4.3
Multivariate Analysis of Variance of Childrearing Values: U.S. Sample

| Effect | df | Childrearing Values | | |
		Autonomy	Conformity	Care Orientation
Social Class	4	13.30***	10.34***	2.80*
Gender	1	5.86*	.05	2.95
Class x Gender	4	2.17	2.52*	.42
Edu as Covariate	1	51.32***	30.28***	9.47**
Model	10	11.94***	8.17***	2.53**

Note: All numbers are F values except for degree of freedom; N = 1,340.

* $p < .05$; ** $p < .01$; *** $p < .001$.

Table 4.4 provides an answer to the question. An examination of the mean scores of the three values by social class and gender reveals that the effect of class on the childrearing values is not identical for American women and men. Among women, there are consistent class differences in the valuation of autonomy and conformity. In general, those who are more advantageously located in the social structure attach greater importance to autonomy than those who are less advantageously located. Women with less advantaged class positions attach greater importance to conformity than others. However, among women, there is no significant class difference in care orientation. Among men, the patterns are somewhat different. Based on their mean scores of the autonomy and conformity values, respondents form three distinct groups. On the one hand, professionals and nonmanual workers display the highest mean scores on autonomy and the lowest on conformity. On the other hand, manual workers register the lowest mean score on autonomy and the highest mean score on conformity. Owners/managers and foremen/supervisors stand in between. Their autonomy scores are not higher than those of manual workers nor lower than those of professionals and nonmanual workers. With respect to the care orientation, the mean score of professionals is slightly higher than that of manual workers as well as owners/managers.

While manual workers' overall low valuation of autonomy is expected, the nondifference found between male owners/managers and foremen/supervisors and male manual workers is puzzling and appears inconsistent with previous research. After all, compared with manual workers, owners/managers and foremen/supervisors are more advantaged in terms of ownership and control over the means of production and control over people. This advantage should give them more autonomy and control at the workplace than others. In addition, job conditions differ between owners/managers and manual workers. While owners' and managers' work is substantively complex, manual workers' work is basically routine. Kohn and his colleagues have argued that occupational autonomy and job complexity explain, in large part, the relationships between social class and childrearing values. Why, then, do male owners and managers in the survey not value autonomy more than others do? One reason could be that this is a diverse class group. Due to the limited information on occupation provided in the WVS, I was forced to lump all individuals who claimed themselves as owners or managers or self-employed into one class. In terms of decision-making

Table 4.4
Mean Scores and Standard Deviations[a] of Childrearing Values by Social Class[b] and Gender[c]: U.S. Sample

	Autonomy		Conformity		Care Orientation		N of Cases	
	M	F	M	F	M	F	M	F
Owner/Manager	0.94 (.91)	1.39** (.96)	1.53 (.85)	1.39 (.90)	0.91 (.63)	1.04 (.61)	116	54
Professional	1.08 (.83)	1.31* (.87)	1.41 (.88)	1.23* (.83)	1.10 (.66)	1.10 (.62)	163	163
Foreman/Supervisor	1.00 (.87)	1.21 (.89)	1.58 (.93)	1.38 (.74)	1.05 (.69)	1.00 (.55)	43	14
Nonmanual	1.11 (.91)	1.02 (.82)	1.37 (.92)	1.55 (.75)	0.94 (.70)	1.03 (.64)	70	211
Manual	0.77 (.78)	0.82 (.70)	1.64 (.85)	1.81* (.84)	0.92 (.66)	0.98 (.67)	316	316
Mean Score	0.92 (.84)	1.07*** (.84)	1.54 (.87)	1.53 (.84)	0.97 (.66)	1.03 (.64)	708	633

a. Standard deviations are in parentheses.

b. Class differences in values are tested separately for women and men. For each value within the gender group (i.e., within each column), the differences between italic entries (higher values) and underlined entries (lower values) are significant at p < .05.

c. Gender differences within each class category are marked by levels of statistical significance as indicated:

* p < .05; ** p < .01; *** p < .001

freedom, there may be some difference between an owner and a manager.

Moreover, social class is a multidimensional typology rather than a unidimensional rank ordering. In terms of ownership and control over the means of production, for example, owners/managers (including the self-employed) are more advantaged than any other employees. In terms of the possession of skill assets and formal education, professionals (even some nonmanual workers) are more advantaged than are many owners/managers. The training and job conditions of professionals may stress autonomy more than the training and job conditions of owners/managers. However, in terms of control over people, managers and foremen/supervisors are clearly more advantaged than owners of a small business and some professionals. In this sense, no class location is the most advantaged in all the aspects in which social class is defined. It may be argued that, in general, owners/managers, who have the greatest control over the means of production and the labor power of others, and professionals, who have the greatest control of skill assets that are vital in production and services, are more advantaged class groups than others. It may also be argued that manual workers are the least advantaged social class.

The overall gender difference in the valuation of autonomy remains, however. In every class category except the nonmanual workers, women desire autonomy in children more than men do. Furthermore, among owners/managers, professionals, and foremen/supervisors, women value autonomy and conformity about equally. Men in these occupations value conformity about one and a half times as much as autonomy. Among manual workers, the patterns of both men and women look essentially similar; conformity is valued twice as much as autonomy. Once again, there is no effect of class or gender on the care orientation.

Why do female owners/managers, professionals, and foremen/ supervisors value autonomy more than their male counterparts? Existing literature suggests two explanations. First, social psychologists argue that people often desire what they don't have. Conventionally, women have been taught to be obedient and submissive and to view women's family roles (as an obedient wife and caring mother) as their primary responsibilities. Although a large and ever-increasing proportion of contemporary women have paid employment, gender socialization, the existence of a segregated labor market, and the biases of employers systematically channel men and women into different occupations: men into positions that exercise autonomy and authority and women into positions that serve and defer to authority. Though women are as likely as men to be professionals and though many female professionals are as committed to their careers as men are, women bear children and are primarily responsible for caring for children and other family members in need of care. As a result, women's employment/career is often interrupted because of maternity leave and other familial responsibilities. In terms of earnings and career advancement, the penalty for employment interruption is greater for professional women than for other women. Role conflict may make professional women feel that they don't have much control in their lives. This sense of lack of control, in turn, may prompt them to desire the ability to have autonomy.

Second, structural constraints differentiate women's employment experience from men's. Existing literature suggests that many women work in sex-segregated occupations in which there is little chance for promotion and upward mobility (Kalleberg and Reskin 1995; Yamagata et al. 1997). Even when women work in the same occupations as men do, they face sex discrimination in employment and advancement (Kay and Hagan 1995). Quite possibly, it may take more determination, independence, and imagination (three value items making up the autonomy value scale) for women to achieve career advancement than for men to do so. Because the male power structure has not welcomed women, women may often need to find their own way (autonomy) to achieve rather than being able to achieve by conforming to the male model. Hence, their own experiences make female owners/managers, professionals, and foremen/supervisors consider autonomy more important than male owners/managers, professionals, and foremen/supervisors do.

In summary, the analysis suggests that there were still class differences in childrearing values in the 1990s, though these differences vary somewhat by gender. When American men and women are considered together, manual workers desire conformity most and autonomy least in children, professionals desire autonomy most and conformity least, and the members of other class locations (owner/manager, foreman/supervisor, and nonmanual worker) fall roughly in between these two groups. When men and women are considered separately, the patterns change. Among men, professionals and nonmanual workers endorse autonomy most and conformity least. Manual workers value conformity most and autonomy least. Owners/managers and foremen/supervisors do not desire autonomy more than manual workers despite their advantaged positions in social structure. Among women, owners/managers and professionals are more likely than both manual and nonmanual workers to desire autonomy. Manual workers, on the other hand, are more likely than others to value conformity. This pattern is consistent with the findings of Kohn (1977). The effects of gender on values vary by social class. Among owners/managers, professionals, and foremen/supervisors, women are more likely than men to endorse autonomy. Among manual and nonmanual workers, women's and men's endorsement levels are essentially the same. The finding suggests that women do not uniformly value autonomy more than men do. Rather, only women with advantaged positions in the social structure tend to value autonomy more than men do. These findings indicate that both social class and gender are sources of value variations.

OCCUPATIONAL AUTONOMY AND CHILDREARING VALUES

Kohn's (1977) theory suggests that people of more advantaged class positions would enjoy greater opportunity to make their own decisions at work. Members of less advantaged social classes would have little or no decision-making freedom in their work. The experience of occupational autonomy would, in turn, affect people's valuation of autonomy and conformity. Specifically, those who enjoy much freedom at work are more likely to value autonomy than others do. Conversely, those who have little control over their own work emphasize conformity in children more than others do.

Is there any evidence to support the claim in my data? Table 4.5 presents mean scores on occupational autonomy by social class. Consistent with the claim, there is a positive association between social class and degree of occupational autonomy. The highest mean score of occupational autonomy is obtained for owners/managers ($\overline{X}$ = 8.64), followed by foremen/supervisor ($\overline{X}$ = 8.14) and professionals ($\overline{X}$ = 7.70). Nonmanual workers ($\overline{X}$ = 6.87) and manual workers ($\overline{X}$ = 6.76) have the lowest mean scores. No gender difference is observed within classes. When men and women are considered separately, the patterns are similar except for the female foremen/supervisors, which is a very small group of respondents (n = 10). This suggests that the nature of the association between social class and subjective occupational autonomy is similar for American men and women.

Drawing on the association of occupational autonomy and social class, Kohn and his colleagues have argued that occupational autonomy (or occupational self-direction, as Kohn phrased it) has a profound effect on people's values and orientations, including childrearing values.

Table 4.5
Mean Scores and Standard Deviations of Occupational Autonomy for Men and Women by Social Class: U.S. Sample

Social Class	Occupational Autonomy[a]		
	N	Mean	SD
Owner/Manager			
Men	80	8.64	1.95
Women	41	8.66	1.57
All Cases	121	8.64	1.83
Professional			
Men	126	7.83	2.08
Women	109	7.56	1.97
All Cases	235	7.70	2.03
Foreman/Supervisor			
Men	27	8.37	1.88
Women	10	7.50	2.01
All Cases	37	8.14	1.93
Nonmanual Worker			
Men	59	7.02	2.53
Women	137	6.81	2.39
All Cases	196	6.87	2.43
Manual Worker			
Men	216	6.84	2.54
Women	99	6.58	2.71
All Cases	315	6.76	2.59
Entire Sample			
Men	546	7.48	2.41
Women	418	7.18	2.35
All Cases	982	7.36	2.38

a. Scores range from 0 to 10.

Specifically, those who enjoy much freedom at work are more likely to value autonomy than others do. Conversely, those who have little control over their own work emphasize conformity in children more than others do. To test the argument, I have examined the relationship between occupational autonomy and the valuation of autonomy and conformity. In my analysis, however, zero-order correlations between subjective occupational autonomy and valuation of autonomy ($r = -.04$) and conformity ($r = -.05$) are very small (results are not shown here). Furthermore, the nature of the correlation between occupational autonomy and valuation of autonomy is inconsistent with the theory; the two variables are negatively related. The findings suggest strongly that occupational autonomy is not the mechanism driving values.

One possible explanation is that the measure in my study does not cover the full range of occupational autonomy. Kohn and his colleagues (Kohn and Schooler 1983; Kohn et al. 1986) measured the occupational self-directness in terms of job complexity, the closeness of supervision, and the routinization of the work flow. Job complexity is a key concept in sociological research on occupations. It refers to the level, scope, and integration of mental, interpersonal, and manipulative tasks in a job (Kalleberg and Lincoln 1988; Miller et al. 1980). Substantively complex work requires initiative, thought, and independent judgment. Closeness of supervision refers to the discretionary content of a job. It indicates how much freedom one has in carrying out one's work. One has limited freedom to use initiative, thought, and judgment if one is closely supervised. Routinization of work refers to the repetitive and predictable nature of tasks in a job (Miller et al. 1979). Highly routinized work requires workers to continuously perform the same work according to set procedures, sequence, or pace and restricts possibilities for exercising initiative, thought, and judgment.

Because of the limitations of measures of occupational conditions in the data set used here, I could not replicate all three dimensions associated with the occupational self-directness indexed by Kohn. My measure of occupational autonomy is based on a respondent's freedom in making his or her decisions at work. While my measure does not capture the substantive complexity or the routinization of work, it is a close replicate of one of the three job conditions in Kohn's measure— the closeness of supervision. It reflects the amount of discretion that a person has in a job role. Although it is limited in scope, it does indicate how free an individual is to use initiative, thought, and independent judgment in carrying out his or her work. In my analysis, however, decision-making freedom is found unrelated to autonomy valuation. This finding is not inconsistent with other research on the relationship between occupational conditions and value orientations. Alwin (1984, 1989), for example, found that occupation by itself was unrelated to parental values. In assessing the effects of work on women's psychological functioning, Miller et al. (1979) also found that closeness of supervision was not associated with any aspect of value orientations. My findings provide additional evidence to support the proposition that decision-making freedom (or closeness of supervision), one of the dimensions of occupational self-directness, no longer directly affects value orientations. If this aspect of occupational autonomy ever conditioned values, there has certainly been a change over time.

BELIEF SYSTEMS AND CHILDREARING VALUES

The findings reported earlier clearly indicate that gender makes a difference in one's desire for autonomy in children. How can we explain women's overall higher scores on the valuation of autonomy than men's? There are two competing explanations. First, social psychological theory suggests that people tend to value/desire what they don't have. Women, in general, tend to feel that they have less control in their lives, and they would value autonomy more than men do. Second, drawing upon feminist theory, I argued that the attitudes toward women's labor force participation would condition the effects of social class on autonomy valuation. I, therefore, expected that the level of support for women's labor force participation would be positively related to the valuation of autonomy in children.

In an initial analysis, I compared the mean scores of sense of control and support for women's labor force participation between women and men. Contrary to the common assumption, there is no gender disparity with respect to sense of control in life (women's $\overline{X}$ = 7.64, men's $\overline{X}$ = 7.56). However, compared with men, women are slightly, but statistically significantly, more supportive of women's labor force participation (women's $\overline{X}$ = 18.82, men's $\overline{X}$ = 18.16, p < .001).

Table 4.6 presents the zero-order correlations between the two attitudinal variables and autonomy and conformity valuation for respondents. These correlations are reported for women and men separately and for the total sample. The table shows that there is little support for a relationship between one's sense of control and the valuation of autonomy. When the total sample is considered, the correlation is very weak (r = .06, p < .05). The statistical significance of the correlation is probably due to the large sample size. When women's and men's samples are considered separately, the size and direction of the correlations remain similar (women's r = .07, men's r = .06). The correlations are positive, but they are not statistically significant. This indicates that, in general, an individual's sense of control in life has no effect on his or her orientation toward autonomy in children. Social psychological theory had suggested a negative relationship between the two variables — that those who feel that they don't have much control in life would desire autonomy more than those who have much control. Thus, this hypothesis was not supported in the U.S. survey data. The measure of sense of control does not have an impact on conformity valuation either. Hence, it cannot be a mediating variable for the effect of occupational autonomy.

Table 4.6
Correlations between Autonomy, Conformity, and Two Attitudinal Variables: U.S. Sample

Attitude Variables	Autonomy		
	Women	Men	All Cases
Sense of Control	.07	.06	.06*
	(764)	(768)	(1532)
Support for Women's Employment	.21***	.12**	.17***
	(646)	(603)	(1249)
	Conformity		
	Women	Men	All Cases
Sense of Control	.00	−.03	−.02
	(764)	(768)	(1532)
Support for Women's Employment	−.26***	−.15***	−.21***
	(646)	(603)	(1249)

Note: Numbers of respondents are in parentheses.

* p < .05; ** p < .01; *** p < .001

Looking at the correlations between support for women's labor force participation and the valuation of autonomy, I found a moderate and consistent positive relationship for women and men considered separately, as well as for the total sample. All three correlations are statistically significant. The correlation between support for women's labor force participation and autonomy valuation is stronger for women ($r = .21$, $p < .001$) than for men ($r = .12$, $p < .01$). The findings confirm the hypothesis. In addition, there is a moderate and consistent correlation between conformity valuation and support for women's labor force participation. The two variables are negatively correlated. The correlation patterns suggest that individuals who value nonconventional roles for women tend to also resist social norms—emphasizing children's autonomy and downplaying their conformity. This is probably because, compared to conformity, autonomy is a less conventional value.

To assess the well-documented effect of religiosity on the valuation of autonomy and conformity, I have also examined the zero-order correlations between the autonomy and conformity value scales and the measure of religiosity. Considerable support has been found for my hypothesis that there is a relationship between a person's religiosity and his or her valuation of autonomy and conformity. As Table 4.7 shows, the level of religiosity is consistently related to the two value scales for both women and men. For women, religiosity is negatively related to the valuation of autonomy ($r = -.27$, $p < .001$) and positively related to conformity ($r = .41$, $p < .001$). The direction and the strength of the relationships are similar for men and women. The relationship between

Table 4.7
Correlations between Religiosity and Valuation of Autonomy and Conformity by Gender: U.S. Sample

Value Variables	Religiosity		
	Men	Women	T Value
Autonomy	−.22***	−.27***	−.24***
Conformity	.40***	.41***	.40***
Number of Cases	762	766	1528

*** $p < .001$

religiosity and autonomy is negative and moderate (r = -.22, p < .001), whereas the relationship between religiosity and conformity is positive and strong (r = .40, p < .001). Thus, my results suggest that the more religious one is, the less one values autonomy and the more one values conformity. Given that religious teachings, in general, preach conformity and convention, the findings are consistent with theory.

To examine the overall effects of the three attitudinal variables on the childrearing values, I next regressed autonomy and conformity values on sense of control, support for women's labor force participation, and religiosity. To explore potential gender differences, the regression models were run separately for women and men. The results of the two analyses are displayed in Table 4.8.

The gender differences in the relationships between the belief systems and childrearing values are observed in the regression analyses. For men, religiosity is the sole source of the two value orientations. The more religious a man is, the more he values conformity and the less he values autonomy. For women, their sources of value orientations vary.

Table 4.8
Unstandardized Coefficients from the Regressions of Childrearing Values on Belief Systems by Gender: U.S. Sample

	Autonomy		Conformity	
	Women	Men	Women	Men
Sense of Control	.034*	.026	−.008	−.030
	(.017)	(.018)	(.016)	(.017)
Labor Force Participation Attitude	.041***	.023	−.047***	−.022
	(.011)	(.012)	(.011)	(.012)
Religiosity	−.053***	−.035***	.075***	.072***
	(.008)	(.008)	(.007)	(.017)
R^2	.115	.051	.206	.166
Number of Cases	640	595	640	595

Note: Standard errors are in parentheses.

* p < .05; ** p < .01; *** p < .001

While the effects of religiosity on the two values are similarly strong for women as for men, sense of control and labor force participation attitude also affect women's childrearing values. Women's desire for autonomy in children is positively related to the sense of control and labor force participation attitude. Their valuation of conformity is negatively related to labor force participation attitude. These results suggest that the greater the sense of control that she feels and the more supportive of women's labor force participation that she is, the more she desires children's autonomy.

In sum, the multivariate analyses have confirmed the relationships between value orientations and belief systems and, more importantly, further clarified gender differences in these relationships that were observed in the univariate analyses. While religiosity is an important determinant of the two values for both men and women, the effects of sense of control and labor force participation attitude are significant only for women. For autonomy values, where a gender gap was observed in earlier analysis, a greater sense of control and support for women's labor force participation lead a woman, but not a man, to value autonomy. In the case of conformity valuation, where there was no gender gap to begin with, there is also a key gender difference in the underlying determinant: support for women's labor force participation depresses conformity valuation among women but not men.

Taken together, these findings suggest that there are some important gender differences in the roots of childrearing values. Moreover, the fact that women's valuation of autonomy and conformity is closely related to all three belief system variables points to pervasive and gendered patterns of social experiences. For men, the relationships between belief systems and values are straightforward; religiosity is all that counts in shaping their values. For women, the relationships are complex; all three variables show independent and direct influence on their orientations toward children. This is probably due to the many dilemmas, conflicts, and complex issues that condition women's lives. The point is *not* that men don't live complex lives but rather that some challenges that women face are unique to them as women—the conflict between family roles and employment roles, sex discrimination at the workplace, and church attendance as an extension of household responsibilities. These issues confront women of all classes. Thus, in multivariate analysis where social class and other factors are taken into account, I expect these belief system variables to continue to affect women's values. However, the effect of social class on men's values, I suspect, will be mediated by the role of religiosity. I test this prediction later in this chapter.

SOCIODEMOGRAPHIC CHARACTERISTICS

Table 4.9 shows mean scores on the three value orientations by age, education, and race. While the measure of age group has no clear effect on a care orientation, it bears a positive relationship to autonomy valuation and a negative relationship to conformity valuation. Age and the two values appear to be linearly related. Younger Americans (18–44 years old) tend to value autonomy more than older Americans (age 45 and older). Older Americans tend to value conformity more than younger Americans do.

The effects of education on the three values are consistent. As expected, the level of education has a positive impact on autonomy valuation, and it has a negative impact on conformity valuation. As the level of education increases, the mean score of care orientation also increases. Overall, better-educated Americans desire both autonomy and a care orientation in children more than less-educated Americans do. The quality of conformity appeals more to less-educated Americans than to better-educated Americans. Thus, the role of education may mediate the effect of social class in multivariate analysis.

For the measure of race, distinctions are made for African Americans, Hispanic Americans, and Caucasians. The three groups show remarkable differences in their childrearing orientations, but the race differences are mixed. For the valuation of autonomy, Hispanic Americans show the lowest mean score (.69), while Caucasians have the highest mean score (1.02). For the valuation of conformity, the lowest mean score is obtained by Caucasians (1.50), and the highest mean score is received by African Americans (1.91). Caucasians also have the highest mean score for the care orientation scale (1.03), followed by Hispanic Americans (.81). African Americans show the lowest mean score on the value scale (.74). In general, African Americans and Hispanic Americans tend to value conformity more than Caucasians. Caucasians, on the other hand, tend to value autonomy and a care orientation more than others do.

In searching for an explanation for the observed racial/ethnic differences in childrearing values, I first compared sociodemographic and other relevant variables between the three racial/ethnic groups. The results are displayed in Appendix C. Among other findings, I found that

Table 4.9
Mean Scores and Standard Deviations of Childrearing Values by Age, Education, and Race: U.S. Sample

Demographic Variables	Autonomy		Conformity		Care Orientation		N	Percent
	Mean	SD	Mean	SD	Mean	SD		
Age Group								
18–24	1.14	.88	1.49	.84	.95	.67	154	9.9
25–44	1.11	.84	1.48	.84	1.01	.65	631	40.6
45–64	.91	.86	1.56	.89	.99	.63	455	29.2
65 and Older	.72	.72	1.75	.81	.97	.64	316	20.3
F Value[a]	19.41***		7.49***		.47		1556	100.0
Education								
Less Than H.S.	.69	.73	1.82	.76	.92	.63	344	24.3
H.S.	.90	.78	1.62	.83	.95	.65	452	32.0
More Than H.S.	1.19	.89	1.37	.87	1.06	.64	617	43.7
F Value[b]	44.81***		33.47***		7.05***		1413	100.0
Race								
African Americans	.83	.76	1.91	.87	.74	.61	166	5.7
Hispanic Americans	.69	.70	1.82	.77	.81	.66	88	10.8
Caucasians	1.02	.86	1.50	.84	1.03	.64	1282	83.5
F Value[c]	9.37***		22.21***		19.14***		1536	100.0

a. Degree of freedom is 3.
b. Degree of freedom is 2.
c. Degree of freedom is 2.

*** p < .001

race is related to age, education, and social class. The average ages of African Americans and Hispanic Americans are younger than that of Caucasians. I had not expected this age difference. African Americans and Hispanic Americans also have a lower level of education than do Caucasians. Finally, racial minorities are much more likely than the white to be disadvantageously located in the social structure. Thus, the value orientations associated with race may, in fact, be explained by differences in age, educational level, and class locations cross the racial/ethnic group. To explore this possibility, I regressed the three value orientations on age, education, social class, and race. The unstandardized regression coefficients are presented in Table 4.10.

The relationships between the sociodemographic variables and childrearing values uncovered earlier were largely reproduced in the multivariate analyses. Table 4.10 shows that sociodemographic variables

Table 4.10
Unstandardized Coefficients from the Regression of Childrearing Values on Sociodemographic Variables: U.S. Sample

Sociodemographic	Childrearing Values		
Variables	Autonomy	Conformity	Care Orientation
Age (in years)	−.009 (.001)***	.005 (.001)***	−.001 (.001)
Education	.165 (.030)***	−.135 (.031)***	.043 (.024)
Social Class[a]			
Manager	.148 (.074)*	−.141 (.075)	−.050 (.058)
Professional	.237 (.063)***	−.231 (.064)***	.080 (.049)
Foreman	.217 (.116)	−.100 (.118)	.039 (.091)
Nonmanual	.136 (.061)*	−.120 (.062)*	.023 (.048)
Race[b]			
African American	−.122 (.074)	.324 (.076)***	−.263 (.058)***
Hisp. American	−.365 (.101)***	.286 (.103)**	−.202 (.080)**

Note: Standard errors are in parentheses; N = 1,397.

a. Manual worker is the reference category.
b. Caucasian is the reference category.

* $p < .05$; ** $p < .01$; *** $p < .001$

play direct and important roles in the valuation of autonomy and conformity. For example, holding other variables constant, race is still a significant predictor of conformity valuation. Racial minorities are more likely than whites to endorse children's conformity. For the autonomy value, while African Americans' lower endorsement is explained by their overall lower class location and educational attainment, Hispanic Americans' lower endorsement is not fully explained by their class, age, and education differences. Moreover, controlling for other covariates, race is most important in the endorsement of a care orientation—no other predictor variable has as strong an effect as race on valuing children's care orientation. Specifically, holding other variables constant, African Americans and Hispanic Americans desire care-oriented values less than others do. This may be due to the unique difficulties that racial/ethnic minorities face in the American society, where racism and discrimination exist. A lower valuation of care orientation could be understood as a means to prepare children to live in an environment of subtle to overt racism. For African Americans and Hispanic Americans who, on average, are much more likely than whites to be hurt in social, psychological, and even physical ways, they may simply believe that a care orientation in children is not important in protecting themselves in this society.

FAMILY STRUCTURAL CONDITIONS AND MOTHERING

In this section, I examine the role of parental status and family size in the three childrearing values. Three dummy variables are constructed to measure parental status. Nonparents are those who have never had any children. Current parents are those who live with dependent children. Past parents are those who no longer have children at home. For parents (both current and past), there are also two measures of family size, the number of children ever had and the number of children living at home at the time of interview. I examine the effect of parental status on values first.

Family structural variables (such as two-parent families versus single-parent families and employed mothers versus non-employed mothers) are known to influence childrearing values, but empirical studies have rarely connected parental status to the valuation of autonomy and conformity. My earlier analyses indicate that age has a negative effect on autonomy and a positive effect on conformity. Since parental status is correlated with age (nonparents are generally younger than parents and current parents are younger than past parents), I predict that nonparents and current parents are more likely than past parents to value autonomy. Past parents, on the other hand, are more likely than others to value conformity. My earlier analyses also indicate that gender, by itself, makes little difference in shaping people's valuation of care orientation in children.

This is not a totally unexpected finding. In recent years, some feminists have argued that women differ from men in their value orientations not because of their sex but because of their life experiences. Building upon this argument, I hypothesized that the social

Table 4.11
Mean Scores and Standard Deviations of Childrearing Values by Parental Status: U.S. Sample

| Childrearing Values | Parental Status[a] | | | |
	Nonparent	Current Parent	Past Parent	F Value
Autonomy[b]	1.07	1.04	.83	11.84***
	(.91)	(.83)	(.91)	
Conformity[c]	1.47	1.55	1.66	5.75***
	(.88)	(.83)	(.86)	
Care Orientation[d]	.99	.99	.98	.02
	(.66)	(.64)	(.65)	
Age (in years)	36.72	41.60	61.90	
	(17.76)	(12.86)	(13.33)	410.46***
Number of Cases	366	695	491	

Note: Standard errors are in parentheses.

a. Degree of freedom is 2.

b. Scores range from 0 to 3; Grand mean is .98.

c. Scores range from 0 to 3; Grand mean is 1.56.

d. Scores range from 0 to 2; Grand mean is .99.

*** $p < .001$

experiences of mothering/parenting render people (mostly women) to be more care-oriented.

To test the hypotheses, I began by running an analysis of variance of the three value scales by parental status. Since age is correlated with parental status, I examine the effect of age at the same time. Table 4.11 presents means of three childrearing values and age by parental status. As expected, parental status is associated with the valuation of autonomy and conformity. Compared with past parents, both current parents and nonparents are more likely to desire children's autonomy. Past parents, conversely, tend to endorse children's conformity.

Gender theory suggests that being a mother predisposes one to value a care orientation. But in my analysis, parental status is not related to the value scale. Because most men probably do not mother (being primarily

Table 4.12
Mean Scores and Standard Deviations of Care Orientation by Women's and Men's Parental Status: U.S. Sample

| Care Orientation | Women's Parental Status[a] | | | |
	Nonparent	Current Parent	Past Parent	F Value
Mean	1.02	1.03	1.00	0.14
SD	.66	.62	.66	
Number of Cases	142	391	228	
Care Orientation	Men's Parental Status[b]			
	Nonparent	Current Parent	Past Parent	F Value
Mean	.97	.94	.98	0.28
SD	.67	.66	.65	
Number of Cases	212	303	257	

a. Degree of freedom is 2; Grand mean is 1.02.

b. Degree of freedom is 2; Grand mean is .97.

responsible for the nurturing and caring for children), the true effects of mothering (mostly by women) might have been diluted in this analysis, which combined women and men. I then ran the analysis of variance on the care-oriented value scale by parental status separately for men and women. For both women and men, parental status again shows little effect on the valuation of a care orientation (see Table 4.12). In my analyses, then, there is virtually no evidence to support the argument that the practice of mothering predisposes parents to desire care-oriented values in children more than nonparents. The lack of evidence to support the hypothesis does not mean that I can reject the mothering theory exclusively, because my measure of mothering is deficient in an important way: it does not assess the actual practice of mothering. But for now, I tentatively assume that mothering, at least as measured here, is not a source that affects people's desire for care-oriented values in children.

Correlations between family size and childrearing values are shown in Table 4.13. While the number of children at home appears to have no effect on any of the three value scales, the number of children ever had is moderately related to the valuation of autonomy and conformity. The negative relationship between the variable and the autonomy value suggests that the more children one has ever had, the less one desires children's autonomy. The positive relationship between the variable and

Table 4.13
Correlations between Family Size and Childrearing Values: U.S. Sample

Family Size	Childrearing Values		
	Autonomy	Conformity	Care Orientation
Number of Children Ever Had[a]	−.11***	.12***	−.01
Number of Children Living at Home[b]	.03	.03	−.00

a. Number of responses is 1,568.

b. Number of responses is 1,567.

*** p < .001

Table 4.14
Unstandardized Coefficients from the Regression of Childrearing Values on Family Structural Variables: U.S. Sample

Family Structural Variables	Childrearing Values	
	Autonomy	Conformity
Parental Status[a]		
Current Parent	.153 (.068)*	−.112 (.070)
Past Parent	.105 (.077)	−.095 (.078)
Number of Children Ever Had	−.033 (.017)	.050 (.017)**
Age (in years)	−.008 (.001)***	.004 (.002)**
Conventionality	−.402 (.044)***	.423 (.044)***
R^2	.093	.075

Note: Standard errors are in parentheses; N = 1,547.

a. Nonparent is the reference category.

* $p < .05$; ** $p < .05$; *** $p < .001$

conformity indicates that the more children one has ever had, the more one values children's conformity.

Parental status and number of children ever had are correlated. To better understand how each of the variables independently affects the endorsement of autonomy and conformity, I next ran a multivariate analysis. Because age is related to parental status and number of children and because conventionality may also be related to the two variables, age and conventionality are included in the regression models as control variables.

The results in Table 4.14 suggest that, controlling for age and conventionality, parental status and the number of children ever had show limited effects on the valuation of autonomy and conformity. While parental status has no effect on the conformity value, compared to nonparents, current parents are slightly more likely to desire children's autonomy. The number of children ever had, on the other hand, is positively related only to the conformity value. The positive relationship indicates that parents with many children tend to emphasize children's conformity more than parents with few children do. Since fertility rates vary moderately by social class, education, and religiosity, I expect that these variables mediate the effect of the number of children ever had in a multivariate analysis. I will test this prediction in the following section.

MULTIVARIATE ANALYSES AND DISCUSSIONS

Given the noteworthy class differences in the valuation of autonomy and conformity, the consistent gender gap in autonomy valuation, and the substantial effects of race and several other demographic factors on the three childrearing values, I ask two additional questions. First, do the class, gender, and racial differences persist when all other predictors of the three values are controlled? Second, do other predictors (some of them covariate with social class, gender, and race) continue to influence the three value orientations when they are considered simultaneously with social class, gender, and race?

To address the questions, I regressed the valuation of autonomy, conformity, and care orientation on all the theoretically relevant predictor variables that I described in Chapter 3. To further explore gender differences in the sources of childrearing values, I repeated the analysis separately for the male and female subsamples.[1] In a preliminary multivariate analysis of the data, several measures were found to be unrelated to any of the three value scales. These measures are urban location (urban vs. rural), the number of children ever had, sense of control, and occupational autonomy. To improve the fitness of the regression models, these measures have been excluded in the final equations. The results of the final equations are displayed in Table 4.15 through Table 4.17. In these tables, I present the standardized regression coefficients in order to facilitate the interpretation of the relative effects of the predictors.

It is apparent in these tables that childrearing values are affected by a variety of factors. Both socio-demographic characteristics and belief systems influence the kinds of traits that Americans desire most in children. The regression estimates point to several conclusions.

First, consistent with my earlier findings, one's belief system remains an important source of variation in childrearing values. Respondents with more supportive attitudes toward women's labor force participation are more likely to value autonomy (for the total sample only) and less likely to value conformity than respondents who emphasize women's

Table 4.15
Regressions of Autonomy on Independent Variables: U.S. Sample

	Autonomy		
	All	Men	Women
Age	−.151 (−.007)***	−.166 (−.008)***	−.137 (−.007)***
Gender	.079 (.135)**	--	--
Education	.141 (.149)***	.142 (.152)**	.120 (.127)**
Social Class[a]			
Owner/Manager	.067 (.179)*	.044 (.101)	.093 (.304)*
Professional	.093 (.190)**	.075 (.150)	.110 (.228)*
Foreman/Supervisor	.037 (.173)	.036 (.136)	.039 (.251)
Nonmanual Worker	.047 (.103)	.075 (.226)	.034 (.066)
Race[b]			
African American	−.027 (−.082)	−.046 (−.133)	−.019 (−.057)
Hispanic American	−.061 (−.239)*	−.028 (−.119)	−.091 (−.335)*
Parental Status[c]			
Current Parent	.076 (.129)*	.138 (.236)**	.001 (.001)
Past Parent	.036 (.067)	.079 (.142)	−.022 (−.042)
LFP Attitude	.072 (.021)**	.069 (.021)	.068 (.020)
Religiosity	−.180 (−.034)***	−.145 (−.026)***	−.213 (−.042)***
Conventionality	−.127 (−.230)***	−.138 (−.252)***	−.125 (−.223)**
R^2	.184	.152	.221
Number of Cases	1,111	546	565

Note: Unstandardized coefficients are in parentheses.

a. Manual Worker is the reference category.

b. Caucasian is the reference category.

c. Nonparent is the reference category.

* < .05; ** < .01; *** $p < .001$

Table 4.16
Regressions of Conformity on Independent Variables: U.S. Sample

	Conformity		
	All	Men	Women
Age	.021 (.001)	−.005 (−.000)	.037 (.002)
Gender	.004 (.007)	--	--
Education	−.086 (−.092)**	−.056 (.061)	−.111 (−.115)**
Social Class[a]			
Owner/Manager	−.045 (−.120)	−.035 (−.081)	−.045 (−.142)
Professional	−.120 (−.245)***	−.080 (−.164)	−.161 (−.326)***
Foreman/Supervisor	−.002 (−.010)	.025 (.097)	−.035 (.122)
Nonmanual Worker	−.058 (.127)*	−.060 (−.182)	−.069 (−.129)
Race[b]			
African American	.071 (.210)**	.069 (.203)	.078 (.234)*
Hispanic American	.019 (.074)*	.006 (.024)	.031 (.111)
Parental Status[c]			
Current Parent	−.064 (−.109)	−.054 (−.094)	−.064 (−.107)
Past Parent	−.021 (−.039)	−.037 (−.068)	−.003 (−.005)
LFP Attitude	−.116 (−.035)***	−.111 (−.034)**	−.112 (−.033)**
Religiosity	.360 (.068)***	.354 (.066)***	.361 (.069)***
Conventionality	.111 (.200)***	.120 (.224)**	.099 (.173)**
R^2	.256	.216	.307
Number of Cases	1,111	546	565

Note: Unstandardized coefficients are in parentheses.

a. Manual Worker is the reference category.

b. Caucasian is the reference category.

c. Nonparent is the reference category.

* < .05; ** < .01; *** p < .001

Table 4.17
Regressions of Care Orientation on Independent Variables: U.S. Sample

	Care Orientation		
	All	Men	Women
Age	−.001 (−.000)	.036 (.001)	−.032 (−.001)
Gender	.050 (.064)	--	--
Education	.050 (.040)	.106 (.088)*	−.008 (−.006)
Social Class[a]			
Owner/Manager	−.030 (−.059)	− .048 (−.086)	−.003 (−.007)
Professional	.041 (.063)	.030 (.047)	.049 (.074)
Foreman/Supervisor	.014 (.050)	.008 (.023)	.024 (.112)
Nonmanual Worker	.005 (.009)	−.000 (−.001)	.003 (.005)
Race[b]			
African American	−.103 (−.229)***	−.106 (−.235)*	−.101 (−.224)*
Hispanic American	−.066 (−.195)*	−.013 (−.041)	−.122 (−.328)**
Parental Status[c]			
Current Parent	.013 (.017)	−.018 (−.024)	.041 (.051)
Past Parent	.007 (.009)	−.015 (−.021)	.028 (.039)
LFP Attitude	−.028 (−.006)	.003 (.001)	−.048 (−.010)
Religiosity	−.082 (−.012)**	−.086 (−.012)	−.072 (−.010)
Conventionality	−.058 (−.079)	−.039 (−.055)	−.087 (−.113)*
R^2	.043	.046	.049
Number of Cases	1,111	546	565

Note: Unstandardized coefficients are in parentheses.

a. Manual Worker is the reference category.

b. Caucasian is the reference category.

c. Nonparent is the reference category.

* < .05; ** < .01; *** $p < .001$

domestic roles. Conventionality also has a relatively strong and statistically significant effect on the autonomy and conformity value scales. Conventional Americans, regardless of their gender, desire more conformity and less autonomy in children than nonconventional Americans. Conventionality also shows a negative effect on a care orientation for women.

Religiosity maintains its significant predicting power for all three value scales. The more religious an individual is, the more he or she values conformity and the less he or she values autonomy and a care orientation. Religion's positive effect on conformity values and negative effect on autonomy values may be due, in large part, to religious teachings about the family and parent–child relationship. Biblical doctrines tend to reject modern changes in the family (and other realms of life) in favor of traditional orientations. While the modern view of children and childrearing emphasizes treating children with mildness and developing their autonomy, the traditional view emphasizes children's strict obedience to parental authority. A common saying is "spare the rod, spoil the child." One of the views held by fundamentalist Christians is that human nature is inherently evil and that parents should break the will of children in order to make them more conforming and less sinful. They believe in "beating the devil out of the child."

Given that religious doctrines, for the most part, preach conformity and the fact that religion appeals more to those who feel more comfortable following others' rules rather than leading, I expected the negative effect of religiosity on autonomy and positive effect on conformity. The negative relationship between religiosity and a care orientation is, however, puzzling at first. After all, most of the major religions teach love, unselfishness, and tolerance toward others. One of the major themes in Christianity is brotherhood—"love one another." Why, then, are devout Americans less likely to endorse care-oriented values? There are a couple of possible interpretations. First of all, religious teachings emphasize a common moral vision. Although denominations differ, all Western religions inculcate their followers with specific moral interpretations of beliefs and behaviors that are said to be the word of God. Since God is believed to be eternal, all-powerful, and all-knowing, the word of God is considered the ultimate guide and authority. In Christianity, for instance, religious teachings emphasize that the Bible is absolutely authoritative in all matters that it addresses. Beliefs and behaviors that do not follow God's will are sins. Thus, for religiously committed individuals, to have faith in God is to obey God.

An offense against moral codes is an offense against God and cannot be tolerated. This kind of religious teaching may lead people to be less tolerant toward alternative moral standards. In fact, within a religious community, value orientations or lifestyles not in accordance with the specific moral standards are not only rejected but also condemned.

Furthermore, religions are exclusive. Although it might be argued that religious teachings promote intergroup tolerance and respect among different peoples, it is a common observation that each religion emphasizes its own legitimacy. For example, the first of the Ten Commandments dictates that one should not worship other gods. Hence, devout people may differ in denominations, but they share a common belief that their own religion and faith are the only right ones. The nature and practice of the religions have a profound impact on people's attitudes and behaviors. A considerable body of research suggests that religion and prejudice are positively correlated. Frequent church attendees, regardless of denomination affiliation, have been found to be more likely than nonattendees to show intolerance for members of unpopular groups such as atheists, communists, homosexuals, and even AIDS victims (Beatty and Walter 1984; Greeley 1991; Hunsburger 1995). Since my measure of a care orientation is made up of "tolerance/respect" and "unselfishness," it is conceivable that these values are emphasized less by religious respondents.

Other literature, however, cautions against the linear relationship between religiousness and intolerance. Some researchers argue that a distinction should be made between religiousness and religious orientation. They claim that religious orientation, not religiousness per se, offers stronger explanations of the negative effect of religion on tolerance (Altemeyer and Hunsberger, 1992; Batson et al. 1993; Kirkpatrick 1993). While religiousness is often defined by frequency of church attendance and religious interest, religious orientation is measured by ways in which beliefs are held and the openness of individuals to changes in those beliefs. Religious orientation distinguishes religious fundamentalism, a rigid and dogmatic way of clinging to one's religious beliefs, from religious quest, a willingness to doubt and question religious teachings. People with either orientation may be active church members. Recent evidence suggests that religious fundamentalism is associated with bigotry and prejudice, but that religious quest is not (Batson et al. 1993). Due to the limitation of religious measurement in the data used here, I was unable to construct religious orientation measures. Caution should be used when interpreting the findings reported here. But the negative relationship between religiosity and a care orientation reported here buttresses the findings of other research (Beatty and Walter 1984; Greeley 1991).

A second noteworthy point is that the effects of sociodemographic variables vary by value dimensions. While age has no effect on conformity and care orientation, younger Americans tend to value autonomy more than older Americans—whether they are men or women. For the total sample, gender also continues to show an effect on the valuation of autonomy. In general, women value autonomy significantly more than men do. This gender gap was reported in previous research but has not been given any empirically based explanation. Results of my initial analysis seem to indicate that a woman's preference for autonomy in children is linked to her support for women's labor force participation. But in the final multivariate equation, this link becomes so weak that the relationship between the two variables is no longer statistically significant for either the female or male subsamples. This finding suggests that support for women's labor force participation does not help explain the effect of gender on autonomy values. Women desire autonomy no matter what attitudes they hold toward women's labor force participation when other relevant variables are held constant.

Do other predictors mediate the effect of gender? Table 4.18 presents parameter estimates and corresponding t-values for the effect of gender on three value scales, first, in models where gender is considered alone (without controls) and, second, in models where gender is considered along with other predictors (with controls). These results show that the effect of gender is largely unaffected by the simultaneous consideration of other predictors. Thus, my findings suggest that, in the case of autonomy valuation, the effect of gender is not attributable to covariation with other independent variables. In other words, gender operates quite independently of other predicting variables. The questions of why women desire autonomy in children more than men do and what factor(s) might better account for women's greater emphasis on autonomy are interesting and important ones. These questions are fertile soil for future research.

Third, in Table 4.15 through Table 4.17, the racial differences in the three value scales hold up in the total sample, but the differences come largely from the racial gaps among women. For example, while men across the racial groups are similar in the valuation of autonomy and conformity, Hispanic women are less likely than Caucasian women to desire autonomy in children. Analogously, children's conformity is a concern more important for African American women than for Caucasian women. This may be a result of structural constraints in black families. Relative to white families, a greater proportion of African American families are headed by single women.

Theory and empirical evidence suggest a positive relationship between single-parenthood and parental valuation of children's conformity. Theory suggests that the presence of a second parent tends to function as a check on the power over children of the first parent (Bronfenbrenner 1979; Gecas 1981). Empirical research supports the argument and identifies unique difficulties that single-parents face in raising children. For example, Thomson et al. (1992) found that the number of partners in a family affected the amount of control over children. In addition, for most single-parents, it is a real struggle to raise children, control them, and provide for them on one's own. Thus, children's conformity may become more important in single-parent families than in two-parent families. Moreover, racial minorities are more likely than whites to live in segregated and poor areas, where the safety of children as well as other residents is constantly threatened. A greater valuation of children's conformity may represent people's attempt to protect their children from danger (and other hostile forces).

Table 4.18
Effects of Gender with and without Controls for Other Predictors[a]: U.S. Sample

Childrearing Values	Without Controls		With Controls[b]	
	Effect	t–value	Effect	t–value
Autonomy	.069	2.731	.079	2.712
	(.117)		(.135)	
Conformity	.022	.851	.004	.149
	(.037)		(.007)	
Care Orientation	.041	1.610	.050	1.584
	(.053)		(.064)	

a. Effects are standardized coefficients; unstandardized coefficients are in parentheses.

b. Controls include age, education, social class, race, parental status, women's role attitude, religiosity, and conventionality.

Fourth, unlike my earlier findings, in this multivariate and gender-specific framework, social class appears to be related to only two of women's childrearing values—autonomy and conformity. Men's values are not affected at all by their class locations, or, more precisely, any such effect would be via different religious or conventionality orientations. However, for both the total sample and the male and female subsamples, education maintains its strong effects on measures of autonomy and conformity. My findings with regard to the importance of education over class are consistent with those reported by Kohn (1977) and Alwin (1986, 1989). There are a couple of possible interpretations of the important effect of education on childrearing values. It is a common observation that one of the major functions of education is to teach people to think for themselves. Higher levels of schooling increase one's intellectual flexibility, and this, in turn, influences childrearing values (Kohn 1977). The further one goes in school, the more likely one is to think for oneself. Thus, educated individuals, having been taught to think for themselves, desire their children also to be independent and autonomous. Education also prepares the individual for work. People's orientations to children may reflect other acquired orientations and dispositions. It has been argued that years of schooling socialize and prepare individuals for different positions in the occupational structure. Successful job performance at particular levels of the production hierarchy requires different personality characteristics and skills that come largely from formal education. However, while occupational positions (or social class) are related to education, in my analyses, the effects of education on values appear to be not mediated by occupational positions, even though both education and occupation are measured crudely.

Previous work by Kohn (1977) and Alwin (1986, 1989) has made much of the fact that, whether one takes the total effects of education as the measure of relative importance or the effects of education net of occupational status, the level of education shows a larger role. My results provide additional evidence for the proposition that while the effects of education operate independently of the imperatives of the job, the importance of occupation (or social class) for childrearing values, at least for American men, may have been diminishing over time.

Finally, as noted in my discussion of the results reported in Table 4-11 and Table 4-12, neither gender nor parental status/mothering has any significant effect on the valuation of care orientation. Although being a current parent has a positive effect on autonomy valuation for men, the status has no effect for women on any of the three values. Across the disciplines scholars have been probing the extent, nature, and roots of differences between women and men. Influenced by inferences drawn from several bodies of theoretical and empirical literature, I began this study expecting to find gender differences among American adults in their valuation of care orientation in children. I hypothesized that being women and mothers would have a positive effect on the valuation of care orientation. Contrary to these expectations, neither gender nor parental status/mothering is related to people's desire for unselfishness and tolerance/respect in children. Rather, religiosity and a racial minority status make a significant contribution to the variance in the valuation of care orientation. Both variables have a strong negative effect on the value scale. For female respondents, conventionality and care orientation are also negatively correlated. The lack of an association between parental status/mothering and care orientation might be attributed to my measure. As I discussed earlier, my measure of mothering is a crude one. Although I used the best approximation that I could get from the data, the measure does not reflect the practice of mothering, as is defined in the "maternalism thesis" (Ruddick 1989). Living with children makes it most likely for one to be a parent, but being a parent or mother does not automatically make one practice mothering—nurturing, protecting, caring for, and sacrificing for one's children.

Because of the crudeness of the measure of mothering in the present analysis, the conclusion that I reached can be considered only tentative. More precise measurement of mothering is needed in future analysis if we are to be more confident about whether the role of gender/mothering shapes people's lives and orientations.

NOTE

1. Alternatively, mechanisms measuring interactions of predictor variables such as social class and gender could be constructed and included in the models. But the coefficients from the gender-specific equations are more intuitive for interpretations.

Chapter 5

Sources of Childrearing Values: Findings from the Chinese Sample

This chapter assesses the relationships between childrearing values and their predictors in the Chinese sample. Hypotheses formulated in Chapter 2 regarding Chinese childrearing orientations are tested empirically. As in Chapter 4, three measures of value orientations for children are examined. These measures are valuation of autonomy, valuation of conformity, and valuation of care orientation. While the measures of autonomy and care orientation are identical to those used in the analyses of U.S. data, the survey items representing the conformity scale in the Chinese sample differ from those in the U.S. sample. Specifically, the American version of conformity measure is made of "obedience," "good manners," and "religious faith," whereas the Chinese version of conformity value is composed of "obedience," "hard work," and "thrift/saving." (See Chapter 3 for an examination and discussion of the value scales.)

Analyses of Chinese childrearing orientations are organized in 6 sections. First I examine the relationships between social class and the three value dimensions. Then I assess the links among social class, occupational autonomy, and the valuations of autonomy and conformity. Next I investigate the impact of other relevant sociodemographic variables on value orientations. Next I analyze the influence of family structure on the values. Then I examine the associations between the independent variables and the childrearing values in a multivariate framework. Finally, I summarize and discuss the findings observed in the previous sections.

SOCIAL CLASS, GENDER, AND CHILDREARING VALUES

Drawing upon the existing literature on command economy and women's high participation in public life, I hypothesized that both social class and gender would have a minimal impact on childrearing values of urban Chinese adults. To test the hypotheses, the three values were subjected to a 5 (Class) × 2 (Gender) multivariate analysis of variance (MANOVA). This analysis reveals the overall relationship among the three values and class and gender. Because education is correlated to social class, the MANOVA model controls for the effect of education. The results in Table 5.1 suggest that while there is no gender gap in any of the three value orientations, there are some class differences in the valuation of autonomy and conformity of Chinese adults. Significant education effects on autonomy and conformity values also emerge from the analysis.

In order to understand how members of different classes diverge in their value orientations for children, I next computed means of the three values by social class. Table 5.2 presents mean scores and standard deviations of the three value scales by social class for Chinese respondents. In terms of the valuation of autonomy, the mean score of

Table 5.1
Multivariate Analysis of Variance of Childrearing Values: Chinese Sample

Effect	df	Childrearing Values		
		Autonomy	Conformity	Care Orientation
Social Class	4	8.50***	8.98***	.80
Gender	1	.35	1.64	1.61
Class x Gender	4	1.15	.61	1.26
Edu as Covariate	1	19.79***	15.12***	.56
Model	10	5.88***	5.51***	1.09

Note: All numbers are F values except for degree of freedom; N = 884.

*** $p < .001$.

foremen and/or supervisors is significantly lower than those of others, suggesting that Chinese foremen and/or supervisors are less likely to value children's autonomy. With regard to conformity, foremen and/or supervisors value it significantly more than members of other classes do. As a confirmation of the results of MANOVA, there is no class difference in the valuation of care orientation. Overall, with the exception of foremen and/or supervisors, Chinese respondents value autonomy more than conformity in children. The greater emphasis on autonomy than conformity suggests that, in contemporary urban China, adults (except for foremen and/or supervisors) prefer independent children to obedient children.

Hence, contrary to my hypothesis, the findings in the analyses suggest that social class is an important source of value orientations in urban China. The class effects on values, however, deviate from what has been observed in the U.S. sample, where manual workers, not foremen and/or

Table 5.2

Mean Scores and Standard Deviations[a] of Childrearing Values by Social Class[b]: Chinese Sample

| Values | Social Class | | | | | |
	Cadre/ Manager	Profes- sional	Foreman/ Supervisor	Non- Manual	Manual	F Value
Autonomy	*1.65*	*1.62*	1.24	*1.73*	*1.57*	11.91***
	(.79)	(.73)	(.71)	(.75)	(.80)	
Conformity	1.09	1.24	*1.59*	1.17	1.30	11.68***
	(.73)	(.75)	(.71)	(.77)	(.83)	
Care Orientation	.96	1.01	.95	.87	.90	.98
	(.69)	(.68)	(.65)	(.65)	(.66)	
Number of Cases	150	98	202	191	343	

Note: Degree of freedom is 4; N = 984.

a. Standard deviations are in parentheses.

b. For each childrearing value, the differences between italic (i.e., higher values) and underlined entries (i.e., lower values) are significant at p < .05.

*** p < .001

supervisors, desire autonomy least and conformity most. How can we explain the unique valuation pattern of the foremen/supervisors in the Chinese sample? In all likelihood, this should not be directly related to their occupational autonomy. Previous research (primarily based on U.S. data) suggests that, due to the amount of control over production assets, skill assets, and the labor power of others, members of different social class locations experience different levels of occupational autonomy. Occupational autonomy, in turn, affects people's desirability of autonomy or conformity. Members of a more advantageously located social class have a higher level of occupational autonomy than members of a less advantageously located social class; thus, the former also value autonomy more and conformity less than the latter. According to this line of argument, foremen and supervisors should not be a group with minimal occupational autonomy, because they are not the least advantaged class by any of the criteria that define social class. As a matter of fact, first-line foremen and supervisors should be more advantaged than some professionals in terms of having control of others' labor power.

OCCUPATIONAL AUTONOMY AND CHILDREARING VALUES

Is social class related to the experience of occupational autonomy in China? To answer this question, I examined the mean scores of occupational autonomy by social class and the correlations between the five class groups and occupational autonomy. The results are presented in Table 5.3. Consistent with theoretical argument and empirical findings from previous research, occupational autonomy does vary by class locations in China. Of the five class groups, foremen/supervisors show the highest mean scores on their own occupational autonomy. Their mean score (7.06) is significantly higher than that of cadres (6.05), manual workers (5.25), and nonmanual workers (5.07). This suggests that Chinese foremen/supervisors have more control in their jobs than others do. As a group, foremen and supervisors also display the strongest positive correlation between occupational autonomy and social class (Pearson's $r = .23$, $p < .001$). If we follow conventional arguments, we should find that foremen/supervisors desire autonomy most and conformity least. But my analysis shows the opposite: Chinese foremen and supervisors value autonomy least and conformity most despite their relatively advantaged class location and the high occupational autonomy that they experience at the workplace. Furthermore, Kohn's theory would

Table 5.3
Relationships between Social Class and Occupational Autonomy: Chinese Sample

| Social Class | Occupational Autonomy | | |
	r	Mean	SD
Cadre/Manager	.03	6.05	2.18
Professional	.10**	6.66	2.06
Foreman/Supervisor	.23***	7.06	2.57
Nonmanual Worker	−.16***	5.07	2.54
Manual Worker	−.16***	5.25	2.73
Total Sample		5.89	2.62

a. Scores range from 0 to 10.

** p < .01; *** p < .001

Table 5.4
Correlations between Occupational Autonomy and Childrearing Values by Social Class: Chinese Sample

| Occupational Autonomy by Social Class | Childrearing Values | | |
	Autonomy	Conformity	N
Cadre/Manager	−.07	−.01	149
Professional	−.12	.09	97
Foreman/Supervisor	−.01	−.20**	194
Nonmanual Worker	.02	.00	189
Manual Worker	.04	−.08	277
Total Sample	−.05	−.03	909

** p < .01

also lead us to expect nonmanual workers to prefer conformity values most and autonomy values least, because, as a group, they have the least amount of job freedom. But the patterns in Table 5.2 show otherwise: Chinese nonmanual workers value autonomy most and conformity least! These findings suggest that occupational autonomy is not the driving force behind the class variations in childrearing values in China.

Table 5.4 further confirms this point. In this table, I display the correlations between occupational autonomy and the valuation of autonomy and conformity by social class. Overall, the associations between occupational autonomy and the two values are very weak. Only one correlation displays modest magnitude and attains statistical significance. This is the correlation between foremen/supervisors' occupational autonomy and their valuation of conformity. Although the two variables are related in an expected direction, all other correlations are weak and inconsistent, indicating that job autonomy does not have consistent and meaningful effects on values for individuals of other classes. Because of the limitation of the data set, I cannot pursue the question further in an empirical way. I provide some speculations later, but for now, I must tentatively conclude that the model of social class $\rightarrow$ occupational autonomy $\rightarrow$ values that articulated by Kohn (1977) is not supported by the Chinese data.

OTHER SOURCES OF CHILDREARING VALUES

Table 5.5 shows mean scores of the three value orientations by age group, education, and conventionality. Age is shown to have a strong effect on the type of qualities that Chinese adults desire for children. The quality of autonomy appeals more to younger Chinese than to older Chinese. The younger a respondent is, the more likely he or she is to value autonomy. Younger respondents (age 18–44) not only desire autonomy more than older respondents (age 45 and older) do, but also value autonomy more than conformity. The quality of conformity, on the other hand, appeals more to older Chinese. The older a respondent is, the more likely he or she values conformity. Older Chinese not only value conformity more than younger Chinese, but also desire conformity more than autonomy in children. Similarly, conventional Chinese desire conformity more and autonomy less than nonconventional Chinese. These patterns support my hypotheses that one's age and conventionality influence value orientations for children.

As in the U.S. sample, the level of education is also consistently related to the childrearing values in the Chinese sample. Education is

Table 5.5

Mean Scores and Standard Deviations of Childrearing Values by Age, Education, and Conventionality: Chinese Sample

Demographic Variables	Autonomy		Conformity		Care Orientation			
	Mean	SD	Mean	SD	Mean	SD	N	Percent
Age Group								
18–24	1.88	.73	.98	.75	.91	.67	161	16.2
25–44	1.70	.77	1.15	.77	.87	.67	440	44.4
45–64	1.28	.72	1.55	.75	1.01	.65	356	36.9
65 and Older	1.11	.67	1.83	.62	.86	.60	35	3.5
F Value[a]	35.94***		33.92***		2.83*		992	100.0
Education								
Less Than H.S.	1.47	.76	1.36	.78	.94	.65	341	38.1
H.S.	1.62	.78	1.24	.78	.92	.68	242	27.1
More Than H.S.	1.76	.76	1.06	.75	.93	.68	311	34.8
F Value[b]	11.87***		12.18***		.05		894	100.0
Conventional								
Yes	1.50	.79	1.34	.81	.93	.66	744	75.0
No	1.72	.76	1.13	.73	.92	.67	248	25.0
T Value[c]	3.93***		-3.77***		-0.17		992	100.0

a. Degree of freedom is 3.
b. Degree of freedom is 2.

* $p < .05$; *** $p < .001$

positively related to the valuation of autonomy and negatively related to the valuation of conformity. In general, better-educated Chinese respondents desire autonomy more and conformity less in children than less-educated Chinese respondents. Education is generally correlated with social class. In the U.S. sample the two variables have been found closely related, and both of them influence the valuation of autonomy and conformity. Bearing this in mind, I decided to examine the relationship between education and social class for the Chinese respondents. At the same time I also wanted to test if social class is related to background variables such as age, gender, and conventionality.

Table 5.6 presents percentage and frequency distributions of selected background variables by social class. The age distribution by social class shows that there are noticeable age differences among the five classes. Although the majority of the respondents in each social class are between the ages of 25 and 64, the proportion of younger respondents (under 25 years of age) in the manual worker class is much larger than that in the other class groups. On average, Chinese workers (both manual and nonmanual) are younger than members of other classes. The mean age of the workers (36 years old for both manual and nonmanual workers) is 10 years younger than that of professionals (46 years old), who are the oldest group. With an average age of 44, foremen/supervisors are a little younger than professionals and a little older than cadres/managers (42 years old). However, they have the highest proportion of people who are conventional. About 85 percent of them adhere to the idea that one should show unconditional respect and love for parents.

Looking at the level of education, we see significant differences among the five classes. While three-quarters of cadres/managers have post–high school education, only less than 11 percent of foremen or supervisors do. The largest proportion of respondents with less than high school education is found among foremen/supervisors (61%), followed by manual workers (52%). Cadres/managers show the smallest proportion of respondents with less than a high school education (5%). Although the high educational level of cadres/managers is consistent with occupational mobility theory and previous research, the low educational attainment of Chinese foremen/supervisors is not. This unique relationship between education and social class can be understood as a consequence of social stratification in communist societies. Evidence from the studies of social mobility in communist societies suggests that, in state socialist countries such as China, career advancement depends on educational credentials as well as political

Table 5.6
Sociodemographic Characteristics by Social Class: Chinese Sample

	Social Class									
	Cadre/Manager		Professional		Foreman/Supervisor		Nonmanual		Manual	
Sociodemographic Characteristics	%	N	%	N	%	N	%	N	%	N
Education										
Less than H.S.	5.3	8	14.3	14	60.5	98	37.1	69	51.7	150
H.S.	19.3	29	30.6	30	29.0	47	26.9	50	28.3	82
More than H.S.	75.3	113	55.1	54	10.5	17	36.0	67	20.0	58
Age										
18–24	6.7	10	1.0	1	8.9	18	12.0	23	30.6	105
25–44	48.7	73	40.8	40	40.6	82	61.8	118	36.4	125
45–64	41.3	62	57.1	56	43.1	87	25.7	49	29.2	100
65 and older	3.3	5	1.0	1	7.4	15	.5	1	3.8	13
Mean years	41.6	150	46.3	98	43.5	202	35.8	191	35.9	343
Gender										
Man	15.0	88	10.2	60	21.1	124	18.9	111	34.9	205
Women	15.7	62	9.6	38	19.8	78	20.1	79	34.8	137
Conventional										
Yes	62.7	94	68.4	67	84.7	171	73.3	140	77.6	266
No	37.3	56	31.6	31	15.4	31	26.7	51	22.5	77

Note: Percentages are computed within a class group for each variable except gender, where percentages are computed across class groups. Percentages may not add up to 100 due to rounding.

loyalty. While individuals with both educational qualifications and political loyalty are often placed in top-level administrative positions, individuals lacking educational credentials but showing outstanding political credentials (Communist Party membership and conformity to party ideology) are often appointed as middle- or lower-level managerial staff—these are usually foremen and supervisors (Bian 1994; Walder 1992, 1995). An interesting and comforting finding in the table is that urban Chinese men and women have similar social mobility patterns. For each class the proportion of men is very close to that of women.

In an effort to explore the overall relationship between childrearing orientations and socio-demographic variables, I next regressed the valuation of autonomy, conformity, and care orientation on social class, education, age, and conventionality. The results are displayed in Table 5.7.

Consistent with the findings observed in earlier univariate analyses, all demographic variables included in the equations show direct effects on the autonomy and conformity values. The effects of age, education,

Table 5.7
Unstandardized Coefficients from the Regression of Childrearing Values on Sociodemographic Variables: Chinese Sample

Sociodemographic Variables	Childrearing Values		
	Autonomy	Conformity	Care Orientation
Social Class[a]			
Manager	.010 (.083)	−.117 (.083)	.026 (.076)
Professional	.092 (.092)	−.068 (.093)	.055 (.085)
Foreman	−.233 (.072)***	.260 (.072)***	−.005 (.067)
Nonmanual	.062 (.068)	−.011 (.069)	−.053 (.063)
Age	−.018 (.002)***	.017 (.002)***	.004 (.002)*
Education	.087 (.033)**	−.071 (.034)*	−.008 (.031)
Conventionality	−.146 (.056)**	.124 (.057)*	.031 (.052)

Note: Standard errors are in parentheses; N = 886.

a. Manual worker is the reference category.

* p < .05; ** p < .01; *** p < .001

and conventionality are consistent and significant. In general, older, less-educated, and conventional Chinese are more likely than young, well-educated, and nonconventional Chinese to desire children's conformity. Conversely, the latter are more likely than the former to prefer children's autonomy. However, controlling for other factors, foremen/supervisors still value conformity more and autonomy less than manual workers. This finding suggests that Chinese foremen's and supervisors' greater emphasis on conformity and less emphasis on autonomy are not entirely due to their older age, lower educational attainment, or conventional outlook. My earlier findings for the relationships between occupational autonomy and class positions indicate that occupational autonomy, at least as measured in this study, is not the source of value variation. What, then, accounts for the general conformity orientation of Chinese foremen and supervisors? A possible explanation can found in the political dimension of foremen's and supervisors' occupational experience. In China, as in other communist countries, the Communist Party promotes conformity as a means of social control and rewards conformity with career advancement. I elaborate on this point in the discussion section in this chapter.

FAMILY STRUCTURAL CONDITIONS

Chinese families underwent important changes in the past several decades. One of the dramatic changes is the shrinking of the family size. Starting in the early 1970s, the Chinese government implemented the "single child policy." This change in family size is related to people's age and may have an effect on childrearing values. Among older Chinese (those who were married and had children before the early 1970s), family size tends to be larger. Younger Chinese adults tend to have smaller families. In large families, maintaining order may become more problematic, and thus parents may rely on strong external behavior control in rearing their children. In small families, parents can devote more time and attention to the needs of each child. For adults without children (these are typically unmarried youth in China), obedience to parental authority may be the least desirable quality, because theory and empirical research suggest that strong disobedience (to any type of authority) is associated with adolescence and early adulthood. If so, we should expect Chinese with no children or a small number of children to value conformity less and autonomy more.

Table 5.8 presents mean scores of three value orientations and age by parental status. As expected, parental status is associated with the type of qualities that people desire in children. Compared to parents, nonparents are more likely to value autonomy more and conformity less. Among parents, current parents (those with dependent children) are more likely than past parents (those with grown children) to emphasize autonomy. Conversely, past parents tend to value conformity more than current parents do. The valuation of care orientation appears to be unaffected by parental status. Age is also related to parental status. Naturally, nonparents are the youngest group with an average age of 24 years. While the mean age for current parents is 43, the average age for past parents is 57. The standard deviations of ages for parents are also larger

Table 5.8
Mean Scores and Standard Deviations of Childrearing Values by Parental Status: Chinese Sample

| Childrearing Values | Parental Status[a] | | | |
	Nonparent	Current Parent	Past Parent	F Value
Autonomy[b]	1.90	1.48	1.14	35.80***
	(.70)	(.77)	(.73)	
Conformity[c]	.97	1.36	1.66	28.80***
	(.74)	(.79)	(.69)	
Care Orientation[d]	.87	.94	.95	.87
	(.68)	(.66)	(.68)	
Age (in years)	23.71	42.73	56.58	
	(6.83)	(11.60)	(11.86)	345.59***
Number of Cases	211	709	59	

Note: Standard errors are in parentheses.

a. Degree of freedom = 2.

b. Scores range from 0 to 3; Grand mean is 1.55.

c. Scores range from 0 to 3; Grand mean is 1.29.

d. Scores range from 0 to 2; Grand mean is .93.

*** $p < .001$

than those for nonparents, indicating a greater age variation among parents than among nonparents.

Correlations between family size and the three value scales are shown in Table 5.9. There are two measures for family size, the number of children ever had and the number of children living at the home at the time of the survey. In keeping with my expectations, family size does represent a structural condition that impacts the kinds of values that Chinese desire in children. Both the number of children ever had and the number of children at home have strong and negative impact on values of autonomy. That means that, the fewer children one has, the more one values autonomy. The valuation of conformity, on the other hand, is significantly and positively related to the two measures of family size. The more children one has, the more one values conformity. The number of children ever had is a stronger predictor for the two value orientations than the number of children at home. Once again, care–oriented qualities are unrelated to any of the two variables.

Although parental status and family size measure different structural conditions in the family, these variables are correlated. To better understand how each of the variables influences the valuation of autonomy and conformity, I next regressed the two values on parental status and the number of children ever had. Number of children at home was excluded in the models because of a collinearity problem. Because family size varies by age and conventionality, the regression model also

Table 5.9
Correlations between Family Size and Childrearing Values: Chinese Sample

Family Size	Childrearing Values		
	Autonomy	Conformity	Care Orientation
Number of Children Ever Had[a]	−.37***	.35***	.05
Number of Children Living at Home[b]	−.22***	.23***	.03

a. Number of responses is 987.

b. Number of responses is 983.

*** p < .001

included age and conventionality as control variables. The results of the regression analyses are reported in Table 5.10. Controlling for other variables, the effects of parental status have become nonsignificant. This suggests that the effects of parental status that I observed earlier have been mediated by other variables in the equations, most likely by age. In fact, parental status is closely related to age; the correlations between the three dummy variables measuring parental status and age range from .31 to .60. Number of children ever had, however, continues to have independent and significant impact on the two values. Specifically, number of children ever had is negatively related to autonomy value and positively related to conformity value. The findings suggest that, regardless of parental status, age, and filial piety orientation, Chinese adults from large families are more likely to desire children's conformity and that adults from small families are more likely to value children's autonomy. These valuation patterns can be seen as people's adaptive

Table 5.10
Unstandardized Coefficients from the Regression of Childrearing Values on Family Structural Variables: Chinese Sample

| Family Structural | Childrearing Values | |
Variables	Autonomy	Conformity
Parental Status[a]		
Current Parent	.012 (.071)	−.058 (.073)
Past Parent	−.177 (.127)	.057 (.130)
Number of Children Ever Had	−.141 (.024)***	.119 (.025)***
Age (in years)	−.005 (.003)	.009 (.003)**
Conventionality	−.173 (.053)***	.176 (.054)***
R^2	.155	.142

Note: Standard errors are in parentheses; N = 987.

a. Nonparent is the reference category.

** $p < .01$; *** $p < .001$

responses to their living conditions at home. In general, the more children in the household, the more challenging childcare becomes. Thus, it is quite possible that parents of large families rely more on parental control in raising their children than parents of small families do.

MULTIVARIATE ANALYSES

Given the significant influence of social class, education, age, conventionality, and family size on the valuation of autonomy and conformity, my next question is, does each of the variables continue to affect the two value orientations when it is examined within a multivariate framework? To answer this question, I regressed the valuation of autonomy and conformity on the predictor variables that have been found significant in the earlier analyses in this chapter. In order to make the China–United States comparison more straightforward, I also included gender and parental status in the regression models. Table 5.11 presents the standardized regression coefficients of the variables included in the equations.

In general, the results mirror what has been found in the previous sections. Age remains an important source of variation in the two values; it is positively related to autonomy and negatively related to conformity. The effects of education are also significant; the less educated endorse more conformity and less autonomy than the better educated. The strong effects of the number of children ever had on the two value orientations are clearly consistent with earlier findings. While youngsters' autonomy is preferred more by adults with no or a fewer number of children, behavioral conformity is desired more by adults with a larger number of children. Perhaps maintaining order in the household is more difficult in large families than it is in small families. Thus, the ability to obey and listen to parents in large families becomes a more important issue than the ability to be independent. Once again, gender and parental status show no direct effect on the two values.

Whether one is conventional or not has an independent effect on childrearing values. Children's conformity is valued more by Chinese who subscribe to filial piety—unconditional love and respect for one's parents. In traditional Chinese culture, obedience to parental and other authority is the first step in carrying out one's responsibility for filial piety. Those who do not adhere to the conventional idea, on the other hand, emphasize more youngsters' autonomy.

Social class also continues to show some effect on the two values. Specifically, compared to manual workers, Chinese foremen/supervisors value conformity more and autonomy less in children. My previous

Table 5.11
Standardized Coefficients from the Regression of Childrearing Values on Selected Independent Variables: Chinese Sample

	Childrearing Values	
	Autonomy	Conformity
Age	−.161 (−.003)	.174 (.010)**
Gender	.010 (.016)	−.031 (−.049)
Education	.094 (.085)**	−.082 (−.074)*
Social Class[a]		
Cadre/Manager	−.017 (−.036)	−.031 (−.065)
Professional	.027 (.066)	−.012 (−.031)
Foreman/Supervisor	−.095 (−.190)**	.105 (.210)**
Nonmanual	.022 (.043)	.015 (.029)
Parental Status[b]		
Current Parent	.027 (.046)	−.040 (−.068)
Past Parent	−.052 (−.188)	−.000 (−.001)
Number of Children Ever Had	−.180 (−.099)***	.172 (.095)**
Conventionality	−.077 (−.137)*	.069 (.122)*
R^2	.158	.145
Number of Cases	887	887

Note: Numbers in parentheses are unstandardized coefficients.

a. Manual worker is the reference category.

b. Nonparent is the reference category.

* $p < .05$; ** $p < .01$; *** $p < .001$

analyses show that part of the reason that foremen/supervisors value conformity is their relatively lower educational attainment, older age, and conventional outlook. But in this multivariate framework where these factors are taken into account, Chinese foremen/supervisors still exhibit a higher level of conformity valuation. As I briefly discussed earlier, this is mainly due to the political screening and the makeup of foremen/supervisors in China. For the past several decades, the Chinese Communist Party has always allocated career opportunities to the loyal in an effort to maintain its ruling. Many individuals with little or no educational credentials were appointed as middle- or lower-level cadres because of their political credentials (Communist Party membership and conformity to party ideology). These are usually foremen and supervisors. Because these individuals achieved career advancement by being obedient and loyal to authority, they may, in turn, value conformity in children to prepare them for upward mobility.

SUMMARY AND DISCUSSIONS

This chapter has examined the relationships between three childrearing orientations and a number of predicting variables in the Chinese sample. I summarize and discuss the major findings of my analyses in this section.

First, contrary to my expectations, childrearing values in China do vary by social class. Although the class differences are not very pronounced and not identical to those found in the U.S. sample, the value patterns of Chinese foremen/supervisors are remarkably consistent and clear. Compared to other Chinese adults, they are more likely to value conformity and less likely to value autonomy in children. While these differences are moderate in magnitude, they persist despite statistical controls for a host of background factors. This indicates that the class location of foremen/supervisors in China has an independent effect on their childrearing values.

What accounts for the class differences in values? Previous research suggests that occupational conditions play a major role in the desirability of autonomy versus conformity in children; those with greater opportunity to be self-directed at work tend to endorse more autonomy and less conformity than those with little opportunity to be self-directed at the workplace. However, my findings in the Chinese data do not support this explanation; the effect of occupational autonomy on childrearing values is very small and inconsistent. Moreover, Chinese foremen/supervisors in this sample have the greatest perception of decision-making freedom at the workplace, yet they value autonomy the least and conformity the most. These findings suggest that occupational autonomy does not explain class differences in child socialization values in China. The class-value theory is, thus, not supported in the Chinese data.

What, then, explains the class differences in childrearing values in the Chinese data? Theory and empirical evidence of social mobility in socialist countries provide a plausible explanation. Theoretical discussions of social mobility argue that, in socialist societies, stratification is organized around a command economy rather than a market economy. In a command economy, the dominant political party monopolizes productive activities. Party elites redistribute revenue and income among organizations and individuals. To maintain its control and promote discipline within its ranks, the party allocates material and nonmaterial resources to the loyal (Szelényi 1978; Walder 1985, 1992). Empirical evidence from the studies of social mobility in communist societies suggests that, in state socialist countries such as China, career advancement depends on educational credentials as well as political loyalty. Although top positions in the occupational hierarchy may require both technical training and conformity to party ideology, middle- and lower-rank administrative positions often stress more the ability to follow party orders. Many studies have documented that local party officials screen candidates for advancement according to political conformity and party membership (Bian 1994; Manion 1985). Because of the limitation of the data, I cannot measure party membership in the present study. But the research of others shows that a considerable proportion of middle-level cadres have party membership (Lin and Bian 1991; Walder 1995). Since a large number of these individuals may have moved up the career ladder mainly because they have been obedient and loyal to authority, it is quite possible that they value conformity in children to prepare them for upward mobility. In this sense, occupational experiences do influence people's socialization values in China; the political conformity of Chinese foremen/supervisors makes them value children's conformity.

Second, respondents' age is consistently and strongly related to their preferences for autonomy or conformity in youngsters. The younger one is, the more one prefers autonomy in children. The older one is, the more one values conformity. This age difference in the values may be partly due to a cohort effect. The social and cultural contexts in China have changed significantly during the past several decades. Confucianism has traditionally been most influential in shaping Chinese culture. Many of the Confucian principles that underlie Chinese families are still in effect, especially ones that affect gender roles in rural areas, but Confucianism's influence on the value and behavior patterns of urban Chinese has declined over time. Most aspects of Confucian teaching were severely denounced during the Cultural Revolution (1966–76). Furthermore, by the early 1990s the society had undergone another "revolution"—the economic reform. China's efforts to rebuild its economy and to modernize the nation involved activities that promoted ideas and behaviors that were more congruent with Western culture— individualism and capitalism. For example, the government issued many policies to encourage a free market economy in which competition is of prime importance. Individual initiatives and success were also encouraged and sometimes even glorified in the mass media. Although the Chinese government does not believe that economic development and modernization require Western-style individualism, its many policies and measures emphasizing competition have effectively promoted individualism.

The value items that make up the conformity scale (obedience, hard work, and thrift/savings) are all qualities emphasized in Confucian teachings. Thus, compared with adults who grew up before the 1960s, adults raised in the 1970s and 1980s are less likely to embrace traditional Confucian values. Instead, they are more likely than older Chinese to prize qualities indicative of modernity and individualism, such as independence, determination, and imagination.

Third, I have found that family size is also related to the valuation of autonomy and conformity. Respondents with a large number of children tend to endorse more conformity in children. Conversely, autonomy is preferred more by respondents with no children or few children. The reason for this is, in part, that family size is associated with respondents' age. Those with a larger number of children tend to be older. Another contributing factor to family size is China's one child policy. The policy was implemented nationwide in the early 1970s but was enforced more strictly in urban areas. It radically affected the way in which age and family size were interrelated in urban families. Those who were married or had children after that time could have only one child. Thus, age and family size are closely related in this survey. But even after I take this factor into account, the number of children ever had still exhibits positive effects on conformity values and negative effects on autonomy values. This suggests that family size is a structural factor that has real and direct impact on childrearing values. In larger families, maintaining order is more difficult, and parents tend to rely on strong control in rearing their children. Therefore, parents with many children may place a higher value on conformity in their children for the purpose of ensuring household order and manageability. The time, patience, and opportunity to explain rules to children and attend to the internal motivations of each child are probably more available to parents with only one or two children.

Finally, as in the U.S. sample, education shows a consistent effect on value orientations. In particular, better-educated Chinese are more likely to desire children's autonomy, whereas less-educated Chinese are more likely to value children's conformity. However, unlike in the U.S. data, where the effect of education is the strongest among a host of other variables, the effect of education in the Chinese sample is smaller and weaker than that of age and family size. Drawing on the philosophy of Chinese education and recent discussions of the relationships between education and social mobility in contemporary China, I offer two possible explanations.

First, unlike in the West, where the teaching of knowledge is the primary goal of education, in China, moral development is the focus of formal education. Confucian education, which has dominated the Chinese curriculum for more than 2,000 years, considers the cultivation of the person (*xiu shen*) as the top priority in education. A well-known Confucian saying is, "From the emperor to ordinary people, the cultivation of the person is the root" (Confucius 1985:1). The cultivation of the person is understood as forming an individual's moral character. In Confucian ethics, loyalty (*zhong*) occupies a central place. Historically, loyalty meant loyalty to one's parents (filial piety) and to the state (the emperor). In this tradition, the main goal of education was to produce obedient sons and daughters at home and loyal citizens of the state. People who failed to possess loyalty were characterized as "lacking education" (*shao jiao*).

Although Confucianism was no longer a dominant ideology in China after 1949, the Chinese Communist Party continued to place moral education at the center of the educational system. The official slogan of education has been characterized in the order of "moral education, intellectual education, and physical education" (*de yu, zhi yu, ti yu*). The function of "moral education" is to foster students' moral character, which has been measured by their loyalty to the party and the state. "Intellectual education" refers to the teaching of knowledge. The government has seen this as potentially dangerous because it may encourage independent thinking. Therefore, political campaigns have been launched from time to time to make sure that students' loyalty to the state is solidly formed and reinforced under the name of "moral education." Those who failed to be molded by "moral education" have been either purged (e.g., the "anti-rightist movement" in 1957) or denied key administrative or academic positions (Davis 1992; Walder 1995; Zhou et al. 1996). In the Chinese political system, each level of leadership is presumably representing the state, and loyalty to the state usually translates into obedience to authorities at all levels. Thus, in China, historically and today, education has always had a political dimension. It has served as a means of maintaining social order by producing loyal and obedient citizens under the name of "moral education." Although the Chinese educational system has not been always successful in achieving its goals, the importance placed on "moral education" has prohibited, to certain a degree, independent thinking. If this is the case, it is quite possible that in China levels of education are not as strongly related to independent thinking as in the United States.

Second, studies of stratification and social mobility in state socialist societies have found that the roles of education in occupational achievement are quite different from those in market economies. In state socialist societies such as China, although education is an achieved status, it has not been always achieved in a system of meritocracy, and it is not consistently related to occupational mobility. During the past five decades of communist rule in China, state policies have varied frequently between competence and political loyalty as a criterion for higher education and promotion. For example, during the years of the Cultural Revolution, political loyalty was either the only criterion or the most important criterion for granting admission to institutions of higher education. Once admitted to colleges or universities, students were judged primarily on their political orientation instead of their academic performance. On graduation, political loyalty was once again the main criterion for job assignment.

On the other hand, many individuals with solid academic records but who lacked political credentials were denied educational or occupational opportunities. Some were even purged for their independent thinking. Many urban intellectuals and their children were sent to the countryside for hard labor in the "anti-rightist" campaign of the late 1950s because they did not obey state policies and criticized the party. Davis (1992) has also demonstrated the occupational downward mobility of children of urban intellectuals during the Cultural Revolution. Similarly, Walder (1995) argues that, even in the economic reform era in which educational credentials have become increasingly important in occupational mobility, political credentials are crucial for entry into administrative positions in China.

Hence, historically, Chinese education did not emphasize independent thinking. More recently, access to education in China changed constantly due to shifts in state policies, and educational credentials did not have uniform effects on social mobility. With these factors in mind, it is not difficult to understand why the effect of education on value orientations is relatively small in the Chinese data.

Chapter 6

The United States and China Comparisons

In Chapter 4 and Chapter 5, the relationships between childrearing values and their predictors are examined at the individual level within the United States and China separately. This chapter focuses on the United States–China comparisons of childrearing values at the national level. Country is the unit of analysis here. Because of the differences in the value structure between the two countries, the 11 value items are compared and analyzed individually. There are four sections in this chapter. First I compare the general value selection patterns of Americans and Chinese. Then I examine sources of national differences in the values. Next I provide explanations of the findings. The last section presents a summary.

VALUE SELECTION PATTERNS OF AMERICANS AND CHINESE

The United States and China are two societies with different cultures. While American culture is centered on the values derived from Judeo-Christian roots, Chinese culture is built upon a value system crystallized in Confucianism. As such, the dominant American cultural themes of relevance stress individual independence and achievement. In contrast, Chinese culture values group cohesiveness and social deference. In cross-cultural studies, American culture is also often considered an individualism-oriented culture, in contrast to Chinese culture, which is said to emphasize collectivism (Hofstede 1980; Triandis 1995).

Drawing on the distinction, I hypothesized that value selection patterns between Americans and Chinese would be very different. In particular, Americans were expected to be more likely than Chinese to desire qualities that have face validity in reflecting Judeo-Christian tradition and individualism. These qualities would be "independence," "determination," and "religious faith." Chinese, on the other hand, were expected to value more than Americans those qualities emphasized in Confucian teaching and collectivism-oriented culture. These qualities would be "obedience," "hard work," "thrift/savings," "unselfishness," and "responsibility."

To test the hypothesis, I first examined the differences in percentages of people in each sample endorsing each of the value items. Percentage distributions of value selection by gender revealed no gender gap in the Chinese sample and a gender disparity in only 2 of the 11 items for the American respondents (see Appendix C). Hence, I focused on country differences in value selections here. Table 6.1 presents the proportion of American and Chinese respondents selecting each of the value items. Percentage difference tests for two independent samples are conducted for each comparison. The results show mixed support for the hypotheses. I discuss the general value selection patterns first.

In keeping with my expectations, significant differences in percentage distribution between the two societies are found for 9 out of the 11 value items. The selection differences of these 9 items between the two countries vary from as little as six percentage points ("imagination"—20.8% for Americans versus 26.6% for Chinese) to as much as 50 percentage points ("religious faith"—51.0% for Americans versus 1.2% for Chinese). However, Americans and Chinese also show great similarities in the kinds of qualities that they desire most in children. One such similarity is manifested in the top 6 value items selected by the survey respondents. Despite the percentage differences between the individual items, American and Chinese adults share 5 out of the 6 value items selected most frequently within each country. For Americans, the top 6 value items in order of preference are "good manners," "tolerance/respect," "responsibility," "religious faith," "independence," and "hard work." For Chinese, the 6 most valued qualities are "independence," "responsibility," "hard work," "tolerance/respect," "thrift/saving," and "good manners."

Looking at individual value items, the between-country differences are both interesting and complex. Compared with Chinese, Americans are more likely to select "obedience" (31.5% vs. 8.6%), "good manners"

Table 6.1
Percentage Distribution of Value Selections in the U.S. and Chinese Samples

Value Items	U.S.[a] %	N	(Rank)	China[b] %	N	(Rank)	Chi-Square
Good Manners	73.8	1162	(1)	52.8	524	(6)	118.57***
Independence	48.1	757	(5)	84.1	834	(1)	334.91***
Hard Work	43.7	689	(6)	64.7	642	(3)	107.22***
Responsibility	68.7	1082	(3)	66.9	664	(2)	.87
Imagination	20.8	327	(11)	26.6	264	(9)	11.76***
Tolerance/Respect	69.2	1090	(2)	61.7	612	(4)	15.38***
Thrift/Saving	21.3	336	(10)	55.5	551	(5)	315.01***
Determination	28.8	453	(9)	44.8	444	(7)	68.51***
Religious Faith	51.0o	804	(4)	1.2	12	(11)	697.21***
Unselfishness	29.5	464	(8)	30.8	306	(8)	.56
Obedience	31.5	496	(7)	8.6	85	(10)	182.65***

a. Number of respondents = 1,575.
b. Number of respondents = 992.
*** p < .001

(73.8% vs. 52.8%), and "religious faith" (51.0% vs. 1.2%), three items making up the conformity dimension in the U.S. data. Conversely, Chinese are more likely than Americans to choose items reflecting the autonomy dimension—"independence" (84.7% vs. 48.1%), "determination" (44.8% vs. 28.8%), and "imagination" (26.6% vs. 20.8%). Two items indicative of Confucian values and the Chinese form of conformity—"hard work" and "thrift/saving"—are also endorsed more by Chinese than Americans (64.7% vs. 43.7% and 55.5% vs. 21.3%, respectively). However, Americans and Chinese are very similar in the endorsement of "unselfishness" and "responsibility." Not only is the ranking of each item roughly the same within each country, the proportion of respondents valuing each item is also similar in the United States and China.

While the greater valuation of "religious faith" by Americans and the stronger emphasis on "hard work" and "thrift/saving" by Chinese are expected, the greater selection of "obedience" by Americans than Chinese and the greater selection of "independence" by Chinese more than Americans are in contrast to the common assumptions. All empirical research on values shows substantial between-country differences. Even countries that are similar in social and political systems, economic development, and cultural/religious traditions display major national differences in human values (Easter et al. 1993; Gundelach 1994; Inglehart 1990). But what is most striking in the United States–China comparison is that the country disparities in the valuation of "independence" and "obedience" are exactly opposite to what the traditional literature has suggested. What accounts for the observed differences?

Could the differences in the value selections be attributed to some background characteristics of American and Chinese respondents? After all, the Chinese sample was drawn from the urban population. Significant urban–rural differences exist in family structure, family size, class structure, and educational attainment in China (Davis and Harrell 1993). In general, rural residents are more likely than urban residents to live in extended families, have more children, be employed in manual work, and have a low level of education. Rural residents are also more traditional in their value orientations. This is the case in both the United States and China (Pan et al. 1994). Given that the U.S. sample contains both urban and rural residents and that the Chinese sample has only urban residents, it is possible that the Unite States–China differences in the values are mainly due to the urbanity of Chinese sample.

Table 6.2
Percentage Distribution of the Selection of Independence and Obedience by Age Group for the U.S. Urban Respondents[a] and the Chinese Respondents[b]

| | Independence | | | | |
| | U.S. Urban | | China | | |
Age Group	%	N	%	N	Chi-Square
18–24	49.3	67	88.2	142	53.60***
25–44	50.6	275	87.1	383	146.23***
45–64	46.4	174	78.7	280	80.72***
65 and over	38.9	107	82.9	29	24.35***
Total Responses	46.8	623	84.1	834	336.94***

| | Obedience | | | | |
| | U.S. Urban | | China | | |
	%	N	%	N	Chi-Square
18–24	30.9	42	5.0	8	35.36***
25–44	29.8	162	5.7	25	91.77***
45–64	33.1	124	13.2	47	40.21***
65 and over	33.1	91	14.3	5	5.14*
Total Responses	31.5	419	8.6	85	175.88***

a. Numbers of respondents = 1,330.

b. Number of respondents = 992.

* p < .05; *** p < .001

My earlier comparison of the U.S. and Chinese samples also shows that Chinese respondents tend to be younger than American respondents. Since age has been found to be negatively related to the endorsement of autonomy within both the U.S. and Chinese samples, it is also possible that the younger age of the Chinese respondents is mainly responsible for the value differences between the two countries.

Table 6.2 presents percentage distributions of the selection of "independence" and "obedience" by age for the whole Chinese sample and the urban respondents in the U.S. sample. The differences in value selection patterns are sustained, however. Although urban Americans of every single age group prefer children's independence (46.8%) to children's obedience (31.5%), Chinese adults of all ages value the former (84.1%) much more than the latter (8.6%). The results, then, do not support the suspicion that the differences in sampling frame or age structure are the only source of value variations between the American and Chinese respondents.

To further probe the source of the cross-national differences in the valuation of independence and obedience, I then estimated, using logistic regression, the effects of three sets of sociodemographic variables, family structural variables, and attitudinal variables on the probability of selecting independence and obedience. The sociodemographic variables are age, gender, race, education, and social class. Number of children ever had and parental status reflect structural conditions in the family. The attitudinal variables are conventionality and religiosity (the second variable relevant for the U.S. respondents only). Analyses were run separately for American and Chinese respondents. Logistic regression equations were used since the dependent variables were dichotomous (i.e., values were selected or not). The two dependent variables are independence and obedience.

For each dependent variable, equations were estimated in three stages of analyses. In the first stage, sets of predictor (independent) variables were entered into equations one at a time. Since there are three sets of predictor variables, three logistic regression equations were estimated, each on one set of the predictor variables. The main purpose was to see how each set of the predictor variables fares individually. In the second stage, the predictor variables were entered together into the equation, but the model dropped the statistically insignificant variables identified in the analyses of the first stage. In the final stage, the model dropped statistically insignificant variables found in the second stage. This analytic strategy was followed in the analyses of both independence and obedience for the U.S. and Chinese data. The results of all logistic regression analyses (standardized and unstandardized coefficients) are displayed in Table 6.3 through Table 6.6.

VALUATION OF INDEPENDENCE AND
ITS PREDICTORS

Table 6.3 shows the logistic regression coefficients from the models of independence value on the predictor variables for the U.S. data. The first column shows the "gross effects" of each of the three sets of the predictor variables. They were obtained from three separate equations in the first stage of analyses. Except for social class and number of children ever had, all other predictor variables are significantly related to the valuation of independence. However, these variables differ in magnitude. Compared with other predictors, the effects of race/ethnicity and parental status are relatively weak. In addition, the dummy variables measuring racial identity show specification effects when considered along with other socio-demographic characteristics. So do the dummy variables measuring parenthood when controlling for the number of children ever had. In the case of race/ethnicity, minority status does not necessarily always depress the valuation of independence. While Hispanic origin has a negative effect on the value, African origin does not. Analogously, the effects of parenthood are not uniform across the board either. While parents living with children (mostly young parents) are more likely than nonparents to value children's independence, parents living without children (mostly old parents) do not.

Model 1 is a full-complement equation because all statistically significant variables from the first column are considered simultaneously in one single model. Here, controlling for other predictors, the Hispanic origin variable no longer shows a direct effect on the valuation of independence. This indicates that the effect of Hispanic origin is mediated by other variables, most likely by the variables measuring belief systems and family characteristics. As Appendix C shows, Hispanic Americans are more conventional and more likely than others to live in households with children (i.e., current parents). Dropping the variable of the number of children has also improved the relationship between parental status and the dependent variable. Now, parents of all ages show stronger desire for children's independence than nonparents do.

Model 2 is a refined, full-complement equation in which the independence value is regressed only on the statistically significant variables found in model 1. All predictor variables show strong and direct effects on the dependence value. The positive effects of education and gender indicate that better–educated Americans and women tend to

Table 6.3
Standardized and Unstandardized Coefficients from Logistic Regressions of Independence on Predictor Variables: U.S. Sample

	Independence		
	Gross Effects	Model 1	Model 2
Sociodemographic Var.			
Education	.155 (.349)***	.156 (.354)***	.158 (.359)***
Age	−.111 (−.011)***	−.097 (−.010)*	−.093 (−.010)*
Gender	.154 (.560)***	.155 (.561)***	.155 (.560)***
Race[a]			
African American	−.001 (−.006)	.008 (.048)	--
Hispanic American	−.079 (−.660)*	−.062 (−.216)	--
Social Class[b]			
Owner/Manager	.038 (.217)	--	--
Professional	.007 (.031)	--	--
Foreman/Supervisor	.027 (.255)	--	--
Nonmanual Worker	.029 (.138)	--	--
Family Structural Var.			
Children at Home	−.035 (−.037)	--	--
Parental Status[c]			
Current Parent	.103 (.374)*	.150 (.545)***	.148 (.537)***
Past Parent	−.007 (−.028)	.099 (.386)*	.101 (.393)*
Attitudinal Var.			
Conventionality	−.142 (−.547)***	−.106 (−.407)**	−.107 (−.411)**
Religiosity	−.135 (−.054)***	−.164 (−.066)***	−.169 (−.068)***
Intercept	--	−.127	−.099
Number of Cases	--	1,360	1,360

Note: Independence is coded as 1 = selected and 0 = not selected.

a. Caucasian is the reference category.

b. Manual worker is the reference category.

c. Nonparent is the reference category.

* < .05; ** < .01; *** p < .001

endorse independence more than less–educated Americans and men. The negative effects of conventionality and religiousness suggest that a traditional orientation depresses the valuation of independence in children. These results largely mirror the findings in Chapter 4, where I examine and discuss the relationship between autonomy and its predictors in the U.S. sample.

Table 6.4 presents the logistic regression coefficients from the models of independence value on the predictor variables for the Chinese sample. Again the first column shows the "gross effects" obtained from the analyses in the first stage. Each set of predictor variables was considered alone in three equations. Among these variables, education, gender, and parental status show no direct effect on the independence value. Of the four predictors that are related to the dependent variable, the number of children ever had shows the strongest effect when the three sets of predictor variables were considered individually. The strong, negative, linear relationship suggests that the more children one ever had, the less one values children's independence. This is also the only variable that exhibits its effect on the dependent variable in the full-complement equations—model 1 and model 2. It mediates entirely the effects of age, conventionality, and class identity of foremen/supervisors on independence valuation. Given that the quality of family life is very much affected by family size in urban China, I had expected an important role of number of children in shaping Chinese adults' behavioral standards for children. But I had never expected that it is the sole source of the endorsement of independence.

My findings in Table 6.3 and Table 6.4 show, therefore, clear and consistent evidence that preference for children's independence has very different roots in the United States and China. For example, sociodemographic characteristics and attitudinal orientations play a greater role in the valuation of independence in the American sample than in the Chinese sample. While the preference of Americans for independence in children is strongly affected by their education, age, gender, racial/ethnic identity, and parental status, as well as their belief system, valuation by Chinese of independence is related directly only to the number of children one has ever had when other variables are controlled. The intercept statistics indicate that the model fits much better to the American data (–.099) than the Chinese data (2.243). There is no doubt that age, class location, and belief systems are linked to the independence value in the Chinese sample; this is manifested in the gross effects in Table 6.4. Since family size is strongly correlated with

age (r = .78) and foreman/supervisor class category (r = .32), the role of
these factors in independence valuation is mediated by the role of family
size—the number of children ever had. Although the correlation between

Table 6.4
**Standardized and Unstandardized Coefficients from Logistic Regressions of
Independence on Predictor Variables: Chinese Sample**

	Independence		
	Gross Effects	Model 1	Model 2
Sociodemographic Var.			
Education	.010 (.021)	--	--
Age	−.163 (−.023)**	.060 (.008)	--
Gender	.089 (.329)	--	--
Social Class[a]			
Owner/Manager	.007 (.036)	−.016 (−.082)	--
Professional	.045 (.259)	.024 (.147)	--
Foreman/Supervisor	−.147 (−.693)**	−.066 (−.295)	--
Nonmanual Worker	.056 (.249)	.072 (.331)	--
Family Structural Var.			
Children at Home	−.228 (−.266)***	−.262 (−.306)***	−.251 (−.293)***
Parental Status[b]			
Current Parent	−.055 (−.219)	--	--
Past Parent	−.043 (−.328)	--	--
Attitudinal Var.			
Conventionality	−.110 (−.460)*	−.082 (−.342)	
Intercept	--	2.232	2.243
Number of Cases	--	987	987

Note: Independence is coded as 1 = selected and 0 = not selected.

a. Manual worker is the reference category.

b. Nonparent is the reference category.

* < .05; ** < .01; *** p < .001

conventionality (or belief system) and family size is not strong (r = .08), the simultaneous consideration of other demographic variables may have diluted the effect of convention. It is a variable that did not have a very strong effect to begin with, barely attaining the significance level when it is considered alone.

VALUATION OF OBEDIENCE AND ITS PREDICTORS

Table 6.5 and Table 6.6 present parameter estimates for models on obedience valuation for the U.S. sample and the Chinese sample, respectively. For Americans, desire for children's obedience is positively related to age, racial/ethnic minority status, religiosity, and conventionality when the three sets of predictor variables are considered individually. In the full-complement multivariate model, obedience valuation is a product of racial/ethnic minority status, religiousness, and a conventional outlook. The effect of age is mediated by other variables. For Chinese, obedience valuation is positively affected by age and number of children as well as conventionality and negatively influenced by cadre/manager status when it is regressed on the predictors individually. In the final multivariate equation, valuing obedience more is a consequence of older age, a conventional outlook, and less advantaged social location. The number of children variable shows no direct effect on the value. This result is in sharp contrast to the finding on the independence value, where the number of children ever had is the only variable that matters. I find this contrast hard to explain. Perhaps this is due to the substantial difference in the endorsement of the two values. While children's independence is considered important by more than 84 percent of Chinese respondents, children's obedience is preferred by less than 9 percent of them.

Unlike the results in Table 6.3 and Table 6.4, which show entirely different sources for the valuation of independence for the two samples, the predictors of obedience valuation are not totally different for Americans and Chinese. In both the U.S. and Chinese models, the endorsement of obedience is positively affected by conventionality. In other words, the more one adheres to filial piety, the more one desires children's obedience. This finding indicates that whether in Western capitalist United States or in Eastern socialist China, obedience is a more conventional value, emphasizing children's respect for parents. Thus, it is preferred more by conventional individuals.

Table 6.5
Standardized and Unstandardized Coefficients from Logistic Regressions of Obedience on Predictor Variables: U.S. Sample

	Obedience		
	Gross Effects	Model 1	Model 2
Sociodemographic Var.			
Education	.065 (.147)	--	--
Age	.069 (.007)*	.055 (.006)	--
Gender	−.041 (−.147)	--	--
Race[a]			
African American	.080 (.491)**	.098 (.579)***	.102 (.602)***
Hispanic American	.101 (.848)***	.079 (.627)**	.077 (.610)**
Social Class[b]			
Owner/Manager	−.075 (−.428)*	−.057 (−.334)	--
Professional	−.054 (−.237)	−.060 (−.268)	--
Foreman/Supervisor	−.018 (−.175)	−.005 (−.046)	--
Nonmanual Worker	−.030 (−.144)	−.040 (−.187)	--
Family Structural Var.			
Children at Home	.024 (.026)	--	--
Parental Status[c]			
Current Parent	−.049 (−.179)	--	--
Past Parent	−.047 (−.184)	--	--
Attitudinal Var.			
Conventionality	.145 (.560)***	.143 (.553)***	.143 (.549)***
Religiosity	.125 (.050)***	.110 (.044)**	.110 (.044)***
Intercept	--	−2.018	−1.852
Number of Cases	--	1,360	1,360

Note: Obedience is coded as 1 = selected and 0 = not selected.

a. Caucasian is the reference category.

b. Manual worker is the reference category.

c. Nonparent is the reference category.

* < .05; ** < .01; *** $p < .001$

Table 6.6

Standardized and Unstandardized Coefficients from Logistic Regressions of Obedience on Predictor Variables: Chinese Sample

	Independence		
	Gross Effects	Model 1	Model 2
Sociodemographic Var.			
Education	−.012 (−.026)	--	--
Age	.211 (.030)**	.208 (.027)*	.269 (.035)***
Gender	.073 (.270)	--	--
Social Class[a]			
Owner/Manager	−.253 (−1.225)*	−.303 (−1.523)**	−.318 (−1.607)**
Professional	−.207 (−1.202)	−.259 (−1.572)**	−.269 (−1.636)**
Foreman/Supervisor	.090 (.423)	−.024 (−.109)	−.015 (−.066)
Nonmanual Worker	−.020 (−.091)	−.108 (−.497)	−.119 (−.546)
Family Structural Var.			
Children at Home	.273 (.318)***	.092 (.107)	--
Parental Status[b]			
Current Parent	−.031 (−.123)	--	--
Past Parent	.037 (.282)	--	--
Attitudinal Var.			
Conventionality	.234 (.981)**	.182 (.761)*	
Intercept	--	−3.985	−4.085
Number of Cases	--	987	987

Note: Obedience is coded as 1 = selected and 0 = not selected.

a. Manual worker is the reference category.

b. Nonparent is the reference category.

* < .05; ** < .01; *** p < .001

However, there are also significant cross-national differences in the sources of obedience valuation. In particular, while class location and age are important predictors in the Chinese sample, they bear no direct impact in the U.S. sample when other variables are held constant. Instead, race is the only demographic variable that influences Americans' desire for children's obedience, and it is a very strong one. I discuss the findings in the next section.

EXPLANATIONS

To sum up, the results of the logistic regression analyses show that the effects of the independent variables on the two childrearing goals mirror largely the findings of the multiple regression analyses of the autonomy and conformity value scales in Chapter 4 and Chapter 5. For American respondents, the probability of selecting the value of independence is significantly and positively related to education, being a female, and being a current parent, and significantly and negatively influenced by age, religiosity, and conventionality. The probability of selecting the value of obedience is positively associated with racial/ethnic minority status as well as religiosity and conventionality. In general, women, young parents, and well-educated Americans tend to value independence in children more than others do. These results are consistent with the findings reported by other investigators (Alwin 1984, 1989; Kohn 1977; Spade 1991; Wright and Wright 1976). On the other hand, nonwhite, religious, and conventional Americans are more likely than others to endorse obedience in children.

My explanations of the effects of these variables on independence and obedience valuation are similar to those discussed earlier in this study. The importance of education in value orientations lies in the functions of education. It is commonly observed that one of the functions of education is to teach people to think for themselves. More years of schooling increase one's ability to do independent thinking and make one value more independent thinking. Women's greater emphasis on independence is likely a result of their life experiences. Despite an enormous increase of women's participation in the labor force in the past several decades, American working women tend to be in occupations marked by sex-segregation, lower pay, and lower prestige. They also receive lower pay even in a prestigious occupational category. In addition, even when women work in the same occupation as men do, they face discrimination in employment and advancement. Hence, women's experiences may incline them, especially those in managerial and professional positions, to believe that it takes more effort for women to get ahead. This belief, in turn, makes them value more independence. The relationships among class, gender, and autonomy valuation reported in Chapter 4 clearly support this speculation. There I found that women in managerial and professional ranks are more likely than others to desire autonomy values—independence, determination, and imagination.

The significance of racial/ethnic status in the American model suggests that majority and minority members do differ in terms of orientation toward children's obedience. I speculate that this is, in part, due to the different social experiences of whites and nonwhites. In general, regardless of their social class and other background characteristics, racial minorities are more likely than whites to live in areas characterized by segregation and concentration of poverty. Living in these areas is less safe and less stable. African Americans and Hispanic Americans may consequently value children's obedience more because it is a way to guard them against the less desirable environment. Furthermore, the greater valuation of obedience by racial minorities may be attributed to structural constraints in minority families. Relative to white families, a greater proportion of African American families are headed by a single, female parent. Empirical research identifies unique difficulties that single parents face in raising children. Single parents—whether female or male—exerted weaker control than two-parent families. Single parents' inability to make demands on children seems to hinge on a lack of support from a coresident adult. The reality that a single parent is responsible for all of the care taking in the single-parent household may force one to emphasize children's obedience at the expense of independence. I speculate that racial/ethnic minority status, especially for African American women, is highly correlated with single-parent status.

The strong effect of religiosity on independence and obedience valuation can be explained by the religious teachings on family relationships. Biblical doctrines advocate that parents have the absolute authority in the family and that children must obey their parents. (See Chapter 4 for a full discussion of the influence of religion on childrearing orientations.)

For Chinese respondents, a very different set of factors is at work. Chinese endorsement of independence is related to the number of children only when the other variables are controlled. All other independent variables appear to have no direct influence on the value. The negative relationship indicates that the more children one has ever had, the less likely that one values independence. This result is consistent with theory that suggests that family size can be a structural factor that conditions the parent–child relationship. In larger families, maintaining order is more difficult, and parents tend to rely on strong parental control in rearing their children. While I expected that the number of children has a negative impact on independence valuation, I did not expect that, in the Chinese sample, it is the only variable that affects the valuation of independence in children. As I discussed earlier, the absence of the roles of other variables such as social class and age is probably due to the strong correlations between family size and class and age.

With regard to the selection of the value of obedience, class locations, age, and conventionality are the significant predictors. While Chinese cadres/managers and professionals are less likely than others to desire obedience, older and conventional Chinese adults tend to endorse the quality in youngsters more than others do.

SUMMARY

As in many cross-national comparative studies in values, my United States–China comparison has found both similarities and differences between the two countries in childrearing orientations. In terms of similarities, one of the striking features is that Americans and Chinese are fairly similar in the kinds of qualities they think important to teach children at home. Among the top six qualities that are emphasized in each country, five are identical. These five qualities are "independence," "hard work," "responsibility," "tolerance/respect," and "good manners." The emphasis of these values by the respondents suggests that certain childrearing goals do not have cultural boundaries.

Another noteworthy value selection pattern is the relative support given to the value of independence versus the value of obedience by the American and Chinese respondents. Although the between-country differences are large, within each country, independence is valued more than obedience. This indicates that for both Americans and Chinese respondents, children's ability to be independent is more desirable than their ability to be obedient. Earlier studies have reported that, over the past several decades in the United States, there is a consistent increase in the valuation of children's independence and a decrease in the valuation of children's obedience (Alwin 1988, 1989; Wright and Wright 1976). My findings provide additional evidence to support this claim.

At the same time, significant differences are found between Americans and Chinese in their valuation of obedience and independence in children. Americans, on average, are more likely than Chinese to think that it is important for children to be obedient. Chinese, on the other hand, are more likely than Americans to believe that it is important for children to be independent. This pattern of value selection does not support the common assumptions and past observations. After all, American culture is known for its emphasis on individualism. Individual autonomy is one of the most treasured characteristics of the American value system. Because of the influence of Confucian teachings on social order and harmony, traditional Chinese culture values obedience and conformity. In the Chinese family, parents have been traditionally concerned that their children's behavior be culturally appropriate and socially desirable. As a result, Chinese children are taught to listen to parents and elders and to follow their guidelines without any objection.

Why are my findings opposite to the expectations? One possible explanation is the differing social environment in the United States and China. The United States is a country made up of immigrants. As a nation, it is characterized by cultural diversity and heterogeneity of norms and values. The greater heterogeneity (in cultural diversity, in values and norms, in behavioral models offered to children, etc.) of the society may undermine the family's ability to circumscribe children's behavior. As parental control becomes more problematic and as child obedience becomes more difficult to achieve, it may also become more valued.

In addition, the United States is plagued by a series of social problems such as crime, drugs, violence, and gangs. In such a social environment, adults may place greater value on children's obedience to parental/external authority because they perceive their environment as a more dangerous place for their children. Indeed, fear is pervasive in the United States (Altheide 1997; Covington and Taylor 1991). Many Americans perceive themselves and their families at great risk for their safety. Numerous public opinion polls show that Americans believe that they live in a very dangerous society and that they are frightened about it. With this mentality, American parents may become particularly concerned with protecting their children and keeping them safe from a potentially harmful environment and influences. A greater value for children's obedience may reflect a greater concern for insulating children from what parents perceive as undesirable or dangerous outside influences. This explanation needs to be tested in future research that controls for fear of crime.

It is often argued that adults may, to some extent, endorse values in terms of how problematic is their realization. Adults may value in children traits that they feel are important and, at the same time, are problematic to achieve in children. Since the diversity of norms and behavioral models offered to children in the United States may make parental control over children more difficult to achieve, American parents may find it necessary to put a greater emphasis on conformity in children.

China has typically been characterized as more homogeneous in terms of cultural traditions and value systems. The influence of Confucianism emphasizing order and conformity to authority often makes us expect that Chinese adults place a high value on children's conformity. While some evidence suggests that Chinese people may be characterized by a more general authoritarian orientation, in the particular area of childrearing values, Chinese respondents appear to be less concerned with children's conformity to authority. I think that this may be because in China parental control and child conformity are less problematic and hence less important to parents and adults. Also, there has been traditionally in China a greater value for self-sufficiency among families. The greater importance attached to the value of independence by Chinese respondents may represent that legacy.

Another way to look at the United States–China difference is to reconsider the caricature of the American value system, a system that may be more "traditional" in character than comparative observers have realized. That is, the relatively higher level of endorsing "obedience" in children by the American respondents, especially by American men, suggests that traditional American culture might be no less authoritarian in terms of parent–child relationships than was traditional Chinese culture. One premise of fundamentalist Judeo-Christian teaching is that the man is the head of the household and has authority over his wife and children. The man should love his wife and children, whereas the wife and children should obey and submit to the man. Up until the latter half of the nineteenth century, most aspects of family law in the United States reinforced the coercive pro-natalism characteristic of paternal patriarchy (Folbre 1987). Parents, especially male parents, had strong authority and power over children, including children's labor. Furthermore, historical studies of societies show that, in the early stage of capitalism, parents had strong legal rights vis-à-vis their children

(Handel 1982; Skolnick 1991). Only after the passage of child labor laws and public education requirements in this century do we see a sharp weakening of parental authority over children in American families. So it is quite possible that in the traditional value system, the idea of children's obeying parents is no less important in American culture than in Chinese culture. The strong positive effect of conventionality (filial piety) on obedience value in the U.S. data provides empirical evidence to support this point.

On the other hand, if we assume that authoritarian values were dominant in both traditional American and Chinese cultures, and if we accept the validity of the measure employed here, the low levels of endorsement of the child obedience are truly remarkable. Even in the United States, where the influence of Judeo-Christian beliefs is still very strong compared to other industrialized nations, fewer than one-third of the respondents seem to value an obedient child. Hence, this may be a traditional value that is on its way out in both China and the United States.

With respect to the high level of endorsement of children's independence by Chinese respondents, one may assume that Chinese are becoming more Westernized in childrearing expectations. A comparison of parental responsibility for children between the United States and China may provide a different explanation. In the United States, children are parents' responsibility until age 18 or when children complete their formal education. After that, parents are no longer obligated to financially support children. Children usually live out of the parents' house, supporting themselves. In urban China, at least until the mid-1980s, the traditional belief in extended family, the extremely low starting wages of young workers, and especially the lack of housing made it difficult for many adult children to live away from their parents' house. Although adult children (whether married or not) share with parents the cost of food and other expenses as well as some household work, in many cases parents feel obliged to do more than their share in all aspects. Feeding, providing for, and taking care of a large, extended family are very demanding economically and physically. In addition, Chinese parents are responsible for furnishing their children's house and providing household goods upon children's marriage. These expenses usually amount to, and may exceed, parents' annual salaries.

Moreover, in Chinese, "independence" is not the opposite of "obedience." It means self-sufficient or self-reliant. To desire children to be independent is to desire them to support themselves. In urban China there is a common perception that children are spoiled nowadays. This is specially so with only children. The only child is over-protected and over-cared for. At the same time, parents are afraid that their children will not be competitive and successful (Xie and Hultgren 1994). In this sense, Chinese respondents' overwhelming preference for independence may very well reflect contemporary Chinese concern about children's ability to be self-reliant.

Chapter 7

Conclusions and Implications

I started the project with the conviction that theory building and theory testing in cross-national comparative studies can be more insightful than in a single-country analysis. With this belief, I set out to examine the structure of childrearing values in the United States and China. Specifically, I sought to answer the following research questions: (1) Do childrearing values form a single value dimension with two opposite poles of autonomy and conformity? (2) Do childrearing values of Americans and Chinese have similar underlying structure? (3) How do various social and personal characteristics shape childrearing values in the United States? (4) How do various social and personal characteristics affect childrearing values in China? (5) Where do American and Chinese childrearing values converge and diverge? In analyzing the WVS data of the two countries, this study has not only found answers to these questions but also, more importantly, presented a clear, yet complex, picture of the structure of childrearing values in the United States and China. Moreover, my investigation makes some contribution to general theory and method in cross-cultural analysis of the consequences of social stratification.

SOCIAL STRUCTURE AND VALUE PREFERENCE

Influenced by Kohn's (1977) class–value thesis, most investigators of child socialization values have focused their attention on the class-linked value dimension of autonomy versus conformity in their examinations of the relationship between social structure and family relations. The theme of a single value dimension is evident in most of the studies. However, several more recent studies have failed to identify a single dimension of autonomy versus conformity. Thus, I started my project by arguing that childrearing values, like any other subject-oriented values, may be multidimensional. My analysis does provide some support for the argument. My factor analysis of the 11 value items in the WVS has identified three dimensions of childrearing values in both the United States and China. These dimensions are autonomy, conformity, and care orientation. The presence of three dimensions indicates the multidimensionality of childrearing values.

My findings also suggest that the underlying structures of childrearing values in the United States and China are quite similar, but they are not identical. This is reflected in the clusters of value items making up the three dimensions of childrearing values in each country. For both the United States and China, the autonomy dimension and care orientation dimension are identical. While "independence," "determination," and "imagination" make up the autonomy dimension, "unselfishness" and "tolerance/respect" constitute the care orientation dimension. However, the items making up the conformity dimension are different in the United States and China. While this dimension is defined by the key item of "obedience" for each country, different additional items add a country-specific conformity tone to the dimension. In the United States the two additional items are "good manners" and "religious faith." In China the two additional items are "hard work" and "thrift/saving." Together with "obedience," they represent country-specific forms of conformity.

Moreover, the value selection patterns of the two countries are quite similar. American and Chinese adults share five out the six value items selected most frequently within each country. These five highly endorsed values are "responsibility," "independence," "tolerance and respect," "good manners," and "hard work." The great similarity of value endorsement suggests that certain child socialization values do not have cultural/national boundaries.

Evident also in the class-value theory is the proposition that autonomy and conformity, as two poles of a single value dimension, are opposite to each other in nature. Many studies have made similar arguments—autonomy and conformity represent two contrasting value orientations and the valuation of one value leads to the devaluation of the other value. Results of my investigation provide scant support for the claims. Findings in my analyses suggest that people who value autonomy may not at the same time devalue conformity. This is specially the case for American women in advantaged classes – female owners/managers, professionals, and foremen/supervisors. They value equally children's autonomy and conformity. One implication of this finding is that, at least for American career women, these two values represent two distinct qualities of children. But they may not be opposite to each other. Hence, both values can be desirable in children.

CLASS/OCCUPATION AND CHILDREARING VALUES

Kohn's theory (1977) suggests that occupational autonomy is the driving force behind value orientations for children—individuals with much control of their work would value autonomy more and conformity less, and individuals with little job freedom would value conformity more and autonomy less. However, evidence from the data does not support these claims.

In the U.S. sample, occupational autonomy is not related to any of the value orientations. This finding is consistent with more recent studies done in the United States (Alwin 1988, 1989). In the Chinese sample, the overall effect of occupational autonomy is not strong either. But there is one exception: those who have more control in jobs—foremen and supervisors—are found to value conformity more and autonomy less than others. This pattern is exactly opposite to the contention of existing literature. Although this is a surprising finding, there are logical explanations for it. Since the Chinese Communist Party promotes conformity and allocates career opportunities to the loyal, status attainment in China is closely related to political reliability and conformity. As a social group, Chinese foremen/supervisors in my data have the lowest educational attainment and are more likely to have a conventional outlook. The theory of the communist political system suggests that they have achieved career advancement mainly because of political conformity and being obedient to authorities (Walder 1985). Empirical studies of social mobility in China support this suggestion (Bian 1994; Walder 1995). Thus, my analysis indicates that while the effect of occupation on childrearing values has become muted over time in the United States, the role of the political dimension in occupational experiences is very strong in China.

GENDER DIFFERENCES

Previous research suggests that child socialization values are affected by a variety of social, familial, and personal characteristics. The results of my analyses buttress the findings of other investigators. However, unlike most previous research that generally pools men's and women's data together, my analyses examined the data separately for men and women and found important gender differences in the structure of childrearing values. For example, while the effect of education mediates the role of social class in American men's valuation of autonomy, suggesting that the importance of occupational experiences in shaping men's child socialization values has declined over time, both education and social class show strong effects on American women's valuation of autonomy. Specifically, regardless of educational level, female owners/managers and professionals are more likely than other women to desire autonomy. Gender differences in child socialization values have been reported in previous research. Controlling for positions in social structure, American women were found overall to value children's autonomy more than men do. However, in these studies, people's positions in social structure were measured by socioeconomic status, a continuous index of educational level and occupational prestige level. In my study, respondents' social positions were distinguished by a categorical class measurement. I have found that women do not uniformly value autonomy more than men do. Rather, only women with advantaged positions in social structure tend to value autonomy more than men do. This finding provides evidence to support the widely held contention that it generally takes more determination, independence, and imagination (three value items making up the autonomy value dimension) for professional (career) women to succeed in their occupational positions. Thus, the different occupational experiences of American women and men explain part of the gender gap in the sources of autonomy valuation.

Similarly, a gender disparity was found in the roots of conformity valuation. While social class and education make no difference in men's endorsement of the value, the two variables play a significant role in shaping American women's desire for conformity. Better-educated and professional women value it much less in children than other women do. A possible explanation for this result lies in the role of socialization and education. Conventionally, gender socialization teaches women to be submissive and obedient. But modern education teaches women (and men) to be autonomous and independent. More years of formal education not only make women less likely to be conforming, but also prepare them for professional jobs. Even though today's labor market is segregated by gender, and many professional women work in female-concentrated jobs such as teacher and nurse, more years of schooling may have made them less conforming than other women.

Thus, my analysis has discovered important gender differences in the effects of education and occupation on child socialization values. These differences are substantial and consistent. They show clear evidence to support the proposition that women and men, due to their different life experiences, vary in the roots of thinking on child socialization issues.

CARE ORIENTATION AND ITS PREDICTORS

Gilligan (1982), Ruddick (1989), and other feminists have asserted that, due to life experiences and mothering/parenting, women and men differ in their value orientations. Specifically, they suggest that women are more likely than men to express other-oriented concerns and to show responsibility for the well-being of others. Guided by feminist theory, I had expected to find a gender gap in the care orientation in the U.S. data. I hypothesized that women are more likely than men to desire care-oriented values in children. However, in my analysis, care orientation is not related to gender, nor is it related to parental status or motherhood. Certainly, my analysis was based on a measure of "mothering" that has limitations. This dictates considerable caution in drawing conclusions here. However, the failure of the gender and maternalist hypotheses in my study urges me to rethink the theoretical promise that these perspectives hold for understanding complex attitudes about raising children. Often, feminist arguments are offered in relatively simple and sweeping terms, underscoring profound and comprehensive differences between mothers and nonmothers in "voice" and value orientations. I believe that the experience of mothering is too rich and varied to be reduced to such simple terms.

In my analysis, care orientation is related to race and religiosity. Racial minorities are less likely than whites to endorse it in children. I had in no way expected this finding and find it hard to explain. My speculative explanation is that the less emphasis placed on care orientation by American racial minorities may be an adaptive response to the unique environment in which they live. Racial/ethnic minorities face much racism and discrimination. Less value for care orientation could be understood as a means to prepare children to live in an environment of subtle to overt racism. For African Americans and

Hispanic Americans who, on average, are much more likely than whites to be hurt in social, psychological, and even physical ways, they may simply believe that care orientation in children is not important in protecting them in U.S. society.

Religiosity also depresses the valuation of care orientation. Given that religious doctrines, for the most part, preach compassion, love, respect, and tolerance, one would suppose that religious respondents desire more care-oriented values in children. But my findings are just opposite to the conventional assumption: more religiously devout Americans are much less likely to endorse care-oriented values. A possible explanation comes from the nature of religious teachings. Although it might be argued that religious teachings promote tolerance and respect among different peoples, there is also a common observation that religious doctrines inculcate their followers with specific moral precepts of God. Since God is believed to be all-powerful and all-knowing, the word of God is considered the absolute guide and authority. Beliefs and behaviors that do not follow God's will are sins. An offense against moral codes is an offense against God and cannot be tolerated. This kind of religious preaching may lead people to be less tolerant toward alternative moral standards. In fact, quite a few studies suggest that religious Americans are more likely than nonreligious Americans to show intolerance for alternative value orientations and lifestyles (Greeley 1991; Hunsberger 1995; Kirkpatrick 1993).

CROSS-NATIONAL DIFFERENCES

Discussions of traditional American and Chinese cultures generally depict the two societies as having very different cultural traditions. While American culture is believed to be centered in the values derived from Judeo-Christian roots, Chinese culture is considered to be built upon a value system crystallized in Confucianism (Pan et al. 1994). As such, American culture is said to value individual independence and achievement. Chinese culture, on the other hand, is said to prefer conformity and group cohesiveness (Bond 1991; Hsu 1981). These generalizations suggest that there should be significant United States–China differences in value orientations. In particular, according to the conventional assumptions, Americans would be more likely than Chinese to endorse children's independence. Conversely, Chinese would be more likely than Americans to desire children's obedience. Once again, my findings are contrary to expectations. I have found that while

Americans tend to value independence more than obedience, they value independence much less and obedience much more than Chinese. Americans' greater emphasis on children's obedience can be understood as a result of the social environment in which they live. As a society, the United States is characterized by diversity in values/norms and heterogeneity of behavioral models offered to children. The greater heterogeneity of values may undermine parental control over children. In addition, many Americans perceive the country as a dangerous place plagued by a series of social problems such as crime, drugs, and violence against children. The sense of insecurity makes them become particularly concerned about their children's safety. As parental control becomes more problematic, children's obedience may become more valued.

General discussions of the American value system have also underestimated the authoritarianism in American tradition. One premise of fundamentalist Judeo-Christian teaching is that parents have absolute authority in the family and the children must obey parents. Up until the latter part of the nineteenth century, most aspects of family law in the United States reinforced parental control over children. Only after the passage of child labor laws and public education requirements in this century did we see a sharp weakening of parental authority over children. Thus, in the traditional American value system, the idea of children's obeying parents is very important.

The greater valuation of independence by the Chinese respondents reflects both a historical tradition and a modern concern. Among Chinese, independence means self-sufficiency and self-reliance. There has been traditionally in China a great emphasis on self-sufficiency among family members. Confucian teachings promote the idea that everyone in the family and/or clan should work hard to be at least self-sufficient. Contributing to the well-being of the family and/or clan is part of filial piety. A person who cannot take care of himself or herself not only becomes the burden of others but also fails to carry out his or her filial responsibilities. Failing one's filial responsibilities is socially unacceptable. Thus, Chinese respondents' greater emphasis on children's independence represents a historical legacy.

At the same time, in urban China there is a common perception that children are spoiled nowadays. Because of the "single child policy," most young and middle-aged urban couples have only one child. The only child is overprotected and overcared for. Parents are much concerned with their children's ability to work hard and compete for educational and occupational opportunities. Thus, Chinese respondents' overwhelming endorsement of children's independence as well as hard work may reflect contemporary urban Chinese concern about children's competitiveness. The economic reform has introduced relatively limited market mechanisms in social mobility process, but professional competence is becoming more important in career advancement. Indeed, in a more recent survey of Chinese urban families, children's competitiveness tops the list of parental concerns (Nan 1998). Within this context, the meaning of independence may be quite different for Chinese and Americans.

DIRECTIONS FOR FUTURE RESEARCH

My discussion points to several directions for future research on the relationships between childrearing values and their determinants. First, in addition to the social, familial, and personal factors considered here, many other factors need to be included in a holistic approach. Due to the limitation of the data, I did not consider the effects of age and sex of children. These two factors have been found to influence the kind of qualities that parents desire in children. In general, autonomy or independence is valued more for older children than for younger children. In contrast, conformity is valued more for younger children than for older children. Moreover, traditional socialization ideals may lead parents to desire conformity/obedience more for girls than for boys.

Furthermore, because of existing and/or potential differences in history, cultural traditions, economic development, and social political system, cross-national comparative studies do need to develop cultural-specific questionnaires, survey instruments, and measures. American scholars constructed the standard interview questions in the World Values Survey largely for the purpose of ensuring cross-national comparability. However, the lack of culture-specific questions at the same time may make the comparison less comparable or meaningful. For instance, a question on the frequency of church attendance measures one dimension of religiousness in the United States, but such a question is meaningless to more than 99 percent of mainland Chinese. Instead, to measure religiousness in China, we should ask questions on the frequency of engaging in rituals of ancestor worship and how strongly people believe in *karma*—that one's behaviors always have consequences in later life and afterlife. Another country-specific question for China is Communist Party membership. It is a very important factor in Chinese social stratification.

Finally, the connection between value orientations and behaviors has not been addressed. The value items examined in this research reflect general attitudes rather than the standards for behavior adopted by a respondent in childrearing activities. There is a difference between a respondent's thinking that it is important for a child to have certain qualities and actually emphasizing those qualities in childrearing practice. Studies that examine both general attitudes and behaviors could identify if there are some links. Such studies will help answer the question of how socialization of the youngsters is carried out in different social-cultural contexts.

Appendixes

Appendix A

Childrearing Value Items

My data on childrearing values come from the following question in the World Values Survey. In data analysis, all value items are coded as 1 = selected and 0 = not selected.

"Here is a list of qualities which children can be encouraged to learn at home. Which, if any, do you consider to be especially important? Please choose up to five."

1. Good manners
2. Independence
3. Hard work
4. Feeling of responsibility
5. Imagination
6. Tolerance and respect for other people
7. Thrift, saving money and things
8. Determination, perseverance
9. Religious faith
10. Unselfishness
11. Obedience

Appendix B

Percentage Distributions of Parental Status by Age Group for the U.S. and Chinese Samples

Parental Status[a]	Age Group							
	18–24		25–44		45–64		65 and over	
	%	n	%	n	%	n	%	n
United States[b]								
Current Parents	25.3	39	65.1	411	45.1	205	13.0	41
Past Parents	2.6	4	7.9	50	45.7	208	73.1	231
Nonparents	72.1	111	26.9	170	9.2	42	13.9	231
Number of Cases	100.0	154	100.0	631	100.0	455	100.0	316

	Age Group							
	18–24		25–44		45–64		65 and over	
	%	n	%	n	%	n	%	n
Current Parents	5.7	9	83.6	367	87.1	310	65.7	23
Past Parents	.6	1	1.4	6	11.5	41	31.4	11
Nonparents	93.7	149	15.0	66	1.4	5	2.9	1
Number of Cases	100.0	159	100.0	439	100.0	356	100.0	35

a. Current parents are parents living in households with children. Past parents are parents living in households without children.

b. N = 1,556.

c. N = 989.

Appendix C

Means and Standard Deviations of Sociodemographic Characteristics and Belief System Variables by Racial Groups: U.S. Sample

	Caucasians	African Americans	Hispanic Americans
Age (in years)	47.70 (17.93)	44.07 (14.84)	39.26 (14.02)
Gender (0=male, 1=female)	.50 (.50)	.49 (.50)	.53 (.50)
Education (1<H.S., 2=H.S., 3>H.S.)	2.24 (.79)	1.91 (.80)	2.03 (.79)
Social Class[a]			
Owner/Manager	.15 (.35)	.02 (.14)	.04 (.20)
Professional	.26 (.44)	.14 (.35)	.16 (.37)
Foreman/Supervisor	.04 (.20)	.04 (.20)	.04 (.20)
Nonmanual Worker	.22 (.42)	.18 (.38)	.13 (.34)
Manual	.33 (.47)	.62 (.49)	.63 (.49)
Parental Status[a]			
Current Parent	.43 (.50)	.48 (.50)	.66 (.48)
Past Parent	.33 (.47)	.27 (.45)	.13 (.33)
Nonparent	.23 (.42)	.25 (.44)	.22 (.41)
Number of Children Ever Had	2.07 (1.67)	2.23 (1.98)	2.36 (1.77)
Conventionality[a]	.65 (.48)	.70 (.46)	.78 (.41)
Religiosity[b]	12.89 (4.64)	14.31 (3.79)	14.64 (3.14)

Note: Standard deviations are in parentheses.

a. Each dummy variable is coded as 1=yes and 0=no.

b. Scores range from 2 to 18.

Appendix D

Percentage Distribution of Value Selections by Gender in the U.S. and Chinese Samples

Value Items	U.S.[a]		China[b]	
	Men	Women	Men	Women
Autonomy				
Independence	41.97	54.73	82.47	86.40
Determination	29.53	27.76	45.87	43.32
Imagination	20.47	21.14	25.97	27.46
Conformity				
Obedience	31.35	31.00	8.09	9.32
Good Manners (U.S.)	73.96	73.41	52.28	53.40
Religious Faith (U.S.)	48.70	53.31	1.69	.50
Hard Work (China)	51.94	35.54	66.61	62.22
Thrift/Saving (China)	23.45	19.33	56.83	53.65
Care Orientation				
Tolerance/Respect	68.13	70.95	59.53	64.99
Unselfishness	28.38	30.87	30.19	31.74
Responsibility (China)	66.71	70.56	68.30	64.74

Note: Culture-specific items in each value dimension are marked by country name in parentheses.

a. Number of respondents = 1,575.

b. Number of respondents = 992.

Bibliography

Abbott, Douglas A., Zheng Fu Ming, and William H. Meredith. 1992. "An Evolving Redefinition of the Fatherhood Role in the People's Republic of China." *International Journal of Sociology of the Family* 22: 45–54.

Adler, Paul. 1986. "New Technologies, New Skills." *California Management Review* 28 (Fall): 9–28.

Altemeyer, Bob, and Bruce Hunsburger. 1992. "Authoritarianism, Religious Fundamentalism, Quest, and Prejudice." *The International Journal for the Psychology of Religion* 2: 113–133.

Altheide, David L. 1997. "The News Media, the Problem Frame and the Production of Fear." *The Sociological Quarterly* 38: 645–668.

Alwin, Duane F. 1991. "Changes in Family Roles and Gender Differences in Parental Socialization Values." *Sociological Studies of Child Development* 4: 201–224.

———. 1990. "Cohort Replacement and Changes in Parental Socialization Values." *Journal of Marriage and the Family* 52: 347–360.

———. 1989. "Social Stratification, Conditions of Work, and Parental Values." Pp. 327–345 in *Social and Moral Values: Individual and Societal Perspectives*, edited by Nancy Eisenberg, Janusz Reykowski, and Ervin Staub. Hillsdale, NJ: Lawrence Erlbaum Associates.

———. 1988. "From Obedience to Autonomy: Changes in Traits Desired in Children, 1924–1978." *Public Opinion Quarterly* 52: 33–52.

———. 1986. "Religion and Parental Child-Rearing Orientations: Evidence of a Catholic-Protestant Convergence." *American Journal of Sociology* 92: 412–440.

———. 1984. "Trends in Parental Socialization Values: Detroit, 1958–1983." *American Journal of Sociology* 90: 359–382.

Alwin, Duane F. and David J. Jackson. 1982. "Adult Values for Children: An Application of Factor Analysis to Ranked Preference Data." Pp. 311–329 in *Social Structure and Behavior: Essays in Honor of William Hamilton Sewell*, edited by Robert M. Hauser, David Mechanic, Archibald O. Haller, and T. S. Hauser. New York: Academic Press.

Alwin, Duane F. and Jon A. Krosnick. 1985. "The Measurement of Values in Surveys: A Comparison of Ratings and Rankings." *Public Opinion Quarterly* 49: 535–552.

Bassin, Donna, Margaret Honey, and Meryle Maher Kaplan, eds. 1994. *Representations of Motherhood*. New Haven, CT: Yale University Press.

Batson, Charles Daniel, Patricia A. Schoenrade, and W. Larry Ventis. 1993. *Religion and the Individual: A Social-Psychological Perspective*. New York: Oxford University Press.

Baxter, Janeen. 1994. "Is Husband's Class Enough? Class Location and Class Identity in the United States, Sweden, Norway, and Australia." *American Sociological Review* 59: 220–235.

Beatty, Kathleen Murphy, and Oliver Walter. 1984. "Religious Preference and Practice: Reevaluating Their Impact on Political Tolerance." *The Public Opinion Quarterly* 48: 318–329.

Belansky, Elaine S., and Ann K. Boggiano. 1994. "Predicting Helping Behaviors: The Role of Gender and Instrumental/Expressive Self-Schemata." *Sex Roles* 30: 647–661.

Belenky, Mary Field, Blythe McVicker Clinchy, Nancy Rule Goldberger, and Jill Mattuck Tarule. 1986. *Women's Ways of Knowing: The Development of Self, Voice and Mind*. New York: Basic Books.

Beutel, Ann M., and Margaret Mooney Marini. 1995. "Gender and Values." *American Sociological Review* 60: 436–448.

Bian, Yanjie. 1994. *Work and Inequality in Urban China*. Albany: State University of New York Press.

Biblarz, Timothy J. *Social Class and the American Family: Differences in Values and Behaviors*. Ph.D. dissertation, University of Washington.

Blau, Peter M., and Otis Dudley Duncan. 1967. *The American Occupational Structure*. New York: Wiley.

Bond, Michael Harris. 1991. *Beyond the Chinese Face*. Hong Kong: Oxford University Press.

Bond, Michael Harris. 1988. "Finding Universal Dimensions of Individual Variation in Multicultural Studies of Values: The Rokeach and Chinese Value Surveys." *Journal of Personality & Social Psychology* 55: 1009–1015.

Bonney, Norman, Xuewen Sheng, and Norman Stockman. 1992. "Gender Roles and the Family Division of Labor at Home and in Paid Work in China, Japan, and Great Britain." Pp. 93–99 in *Families: East and West*, vol. 1, edited by P. L. Linn et al. Indianapolis: University of Indianapolis Press.

Bronfenbrenner, Urie. 1979. *The Ecology of Human Development: Experiments by Nature and Design*. Cambridge: Harvard University Press.

————. 1958. "Socialization and Social Class through Time and Space." Pp. 400–425 in *Readings in Social Psychology*, edited by Eleanor E. Maccoby, Theodore M. Newcomb, and Eugene L. Hartley. New York: Holt, Rinehart, and Winston.

Burns, A., R. Homel, and J. Goodnow. 1984. "Conditions of Life and Parental Values." *Australian Journal of Psychology* 36: 219–237.

Chao, Ruth K. 1996. "Chinese and European American Mothers' Beliefs about the Role of Parenting in Children's School Success." *Journal of Cross-Cultural Psychology* 27: 403–423.

Chen, Chuansheng. 1992. *Paths to Achievement: A Study of Family Influence on Children's Achievement in China and the United States*. Ph.D. dissertation, University of Michigan.

Chen, Chuansheng, and David H. Uttal. 1988. "Cultural Values, Parents' Beliefs, and Children's Achievement in the United States and China." *Human Development* 31: 351–358.

Cheng, Chung-Ying. 1987. "On Confucian Ethics of Modernization and Modernization of Confucian Ethics." Pp. 99–109 in *Confucianism and Modernization: A Symposium*, edited by Joseph P. L. Jiang. Taiwan: Freedom Council.

Cherlin, Andrew J. 1999. *Public and Private Families*. 2nd ed. Boston: McGraw-Hill.

China Daily. November 11, 1994, p. 4.

China's Population Census Office and State Statistical Bureau. 1993. *Tabulation on the 1990 Population Census of the People's Republic of China*. Beijing, China: China Statistics Press.

Chu, Godwin C. 1985. "The Emergence of the New Chinese Culture." Pp. 15–27 in *Chinese Culture and Mental Health*, edited by Wen-Shing Tseng and David Y. H. Wu. Orlando, FL: Academic Press.

Clement, Grade. 1996. *Care, Autonomy, and Justice*. Boulder, CO: Westview Press.

Cohn, Lawrence D. 1991. "Sex Differences in the Course of Personality Development: A Meta-Analysis." *Psychological Bulletin* 109: 252–266.

Confucius. 1985. *The Great Learning*. Beijing: Chinese Bookstore Press.

Conover, Pamela Johnston. 1988. "Feminists and the Gender Gap." *The Journal of Politics* 50: 985–1010.

Conover, Pamela Johnston, and Virginia Sapiro. 1993. "Gender, Feminist Consciousness, and War." *American Journal of Political Science* 37: 1079–1099.

Cook, Fay Lomax. 1979. *Who Should Be Helped?* Beverly Hills, CA: Sage.

Covington, Jeanette, and Ralph B. Taylor. 1991. "Fear of Crime in Urban Residential Neighborhoods: Implications of Between- and Within-Neighborhood Sources for Current Models." *The Sociological Quarterly* 32: 231–249.

Crouter, Ann C., and Beth Manke. 1994. "The Changing American Workplace: Implications for Individuals and Families." *Family Relations* 43: 117–124.

Dahrendorf, Ralf. 1959. *Class and Class Conflict in Industrial Society*. Stanford, CA: Stanford University Press.

Davis, Deborah. 1992. "Skidding Downward Mobility among Children of the Maoist Middle Class." *Modern China* 18: 410–437.

Davis, Deborah, and Stevan Harrell. 1993. *Chinese Families in the Post-Mao Era*. Berleley: University of California Press.

Davis, James A. 1982. "Achievement Variables and Class Cultures: Family, Schooling, Job, and Forty-nine Dependent Variables in the Cumulative GSS." *American Sociological Review* 47: 569–586.

Dietz, Mary G. 1985. "Citizenship with a Feminist Face: The Problem with Maternal Thinking." *Political Theory* 13: 19–35.

Dimaggio, Paul. 1994. "Social Stratification, Life-Style, and Social Cognition." Pp. 458–465 in *Social Stratification: Class, Race & Gender in Sociological Perspective*, edited by David B. Grusky. Boulder, CO: Westview Press.

Duvall, Evelyn M. 1946. "Conceptions of Parenthood." *American Journal of Sociology* 52: 193–203.

Eagly, Alice H. 1987. *Sex Differences in Social Behavior: A Social-Role Interpretation*. Hillsdale, NJ: Lawrence Erlbaum Associates.

Ebrey, Patricia. 1990. "Women, Marriage, and the Family in Chinese History." Pp. 197–223 in *Heritage of China: Contemporary Perspectives on Chinese Civilization*, edited by Paul S. Ropp. Berkeley: University of California Press.

Eisenberg, Nancy, Richard Fabes, and Cindy Shea. 1989. "Gender Differences in Empathy and Prosocial Moral Reasoning: Empirical Investigations." Pp. 7–143 in *Who Cares? Theory, Research, and Educational Implications of the Ethic of Care*, edited by Mary M. Brabeck. New York: Praeger.

Elkin, Frederick, and Gerald Handel. 1989. *The Child & Society: The Process of Socialization*. 5th ed. New York: Random House.

Ellis, Godfrey J., Gary R. Lee, and Larry R. Petersen. 1978. "Supervision and Conformity: A Cross-Cultural Analysis of Parental Socialization Values." *American Journal of Sociology* 84: 386–403.

Ellis, Godfrey J., and Larry R. Petersen. 1992. "Socialization Values and Parental Control Techniques: A Cross-Cultural Analysis of Child-Rearing." *Journal of Comparative Family Studies* 23: 39–54.

Ellison, Christopher G., and Darren E. Sherkat. 1993. "Obedience and Autonomy: Religion and Parental Values Reconsidered." *Journal for the Scientific Study of Religion* 32: 313–329.

Elshtain, Jean Bethke. 1981. *Public Man, Private Women*. Princeton, NJ: Princeton University Press.

England, Paula, Melissa S. Herbert, Barbara Stanek Kilbourne, Lori L. Reid, and Lori McCreary Megdal. 1994. "The Gendered Valuation of Occupations and Skills: Earnings in 1980 Census Occupations." *Social Forces* 73: 65–99.

Ester, Peter, Lock Halman, and Ruud De More. 1993. *The Individualizing Society: Value Change in Europe and North America*. Tilburg: Tilburg University Press.

Evans, M. D. R., Jonathan Kelley, and Tamas Kolosi. 1992. "Images of Class." *American Sociological Review* 57: 461–482.

Feather, N. T. 1994. "Values and National Identification: Australian Evidence." *Australian Journal of Psychology* 46: 35–40.

Feather, N. T. 1975. "Value Systems and Delinquency: Parental and Generational Discrepancies in Value Systems for Delinquent and Non-Delinquent Boys." *The British Journal of Social and Clinical Psychology* 14: 117–129.

Featherman, David L., and Robert M. Hauser. 1984. "Comparative Social Mobility Revisited: Models of Convergence and Divergence in 16 Countries." *American Sociological Review* 49: 19–38.

Featherman, David L., and Robert M. Hauser. 1978. *Opportunity and Change*. New York: Academic Press.

Ferree, Myra Marx. 1990. "Beyond Separate Spheres: Feminism and Family Research." *Journal of Marriage and the Family* 52: 866–884.

Fliegelman, Fay. 1993. *Declaring Independence: Jefferson, Natural Language & the Culture of Performance*. Stanford, CA: Stanford University Press.

Folbre, Nancy. 1987. "The Pauperization of Motherhood: Patriarchy and Public Policy in the United States." Pp. 491–511 in *Families and Work*, edited by Naomi Gerstel and Harriet Engel Gross. Philadelphia: Temple University Press.

Gagliani, Giorgio. 1981. "How Many Working Classes?" *American Journal of Sociology* 87: 259–285.

Gallup, George, Jr. 1990. *Religion in America*. Princeton, NJ: Princeton Religion Research Center.

Gao, Yuan. 1987. *Born Red: A Chronicle of the Cultural Revolution*. Stanford, CA: Stanford University Press.

Gecas, Viktor. 1979. "The Influence of Social Class on Socialization." Pp. 365–404 in *Contemporary Theories about the Family*, vol. 1, edited by Wesley R. Burr, Reuben Hill, F. Ivan Nye, and Ira Reiss. New York: Free Press.

Gerstel, Naomi, and Harriet Engel Gross (eds.). 1987. *Families and Work*. Philadelphia: Temple University Press.

Giddens, Anthony. 1973. *The Class Structure of Advanced Societies*. New York: HarperCollins.

Gilligan, Carol. 1982. *In a Different Voice: Psychological Theory and the Sociology of Gender*. Cambridge: Harvard University Press.

Gilligan, Carol, and J. Attanucci. 1988. "Two Moral Orientations: Gender Differences and Similarities." *Merrill-Palmer Quarterly* 34: 223–237.

Greeley, Andrew M. 1991. "Religion and Attitudes towards AIDS Policy." *Sociology and Social Research* 75: 126–132.

Grimm-Thomas, Karen, and Maureen Perry-Jenkins. 1994. "All in a Day's Work: Job Experiences, Self-Esteem, and Fathering in Working-Class Families." *Family Relations* 43: 174–181.

Gundelach, Peter. 1994. "National Value Differences: Modernization or Institutionalization?" *International Journal of Comparative Studies* 35: 37–58.

Handel, Gerald. 1982. *Social Welfare in Western Society*. New York: Random House.

Herberg, Will. 1967. "Religion in a Secularized Society: The New Shape of Religion in America." Pp. 470–481 in *The Sociology of Religion: An Anthology*, edited by Richard D. Knudten. New York: Appleton-Century-Crofts.

Herring, Cedric, and Karen Rose Wilson-Sadberry. 1993. "Preference or Necessity? Changing Work Roles of Black and White Women, 1973–1990." *Journal of Marriage and the Family* 55: 314-325.

Ho, David Y. H. 1989. "Continuity and Variation in Chinese Patterns of Socialization." *Journal of Marriage and the Family* 51: 149–163.

———. 1986. "Chinese Patterns of Socialization: A Critical Review." Pp. 1–37 in *The Psychology of the Chinese People*, edited by Micheal H. Bond. Hong Kong: Oxford University Press.

Ho, David Y. H., and T. K. Kang. 1984. "Intergenerational Comparisons of Child-Rearing Attitudes and Practices in Hong Kong." *Developmental Psychology* 20: 1004–1016.

Hofstede, Geert H. 1980. *Culture's Consequences: International Differences in Work-Related Values*. Beverly Hills, CA: Sage.

Honig, Emily, and Gail Hershatter. 1988. *Personal Voices: Chinese Women in the 1980's*. Stanford, CA: Stanford University Press.

House, James S., Debra Umberson, and Karl R. Landis. 1988. "Structures and Processes of Social Support." *Annual Review of Sociology* 14: 293–318.

Hsiao Ching. 1992. Annotated by Lai Yanyuan and Huang Junlang. Taiwan: San Min Publishing House (in Chinese).

Hsieh, Kuang-Hua, and Robert L. Burgess. 1994. "Marital Role Attitudes and Expected Role Behaviors of College Youth in Mainland China and Taiwan." *Journal of Family Issues* 15: 403–423.

Hsu, Francis L. K. 1981. *Americans and Chinese: Passage to Differences*. 3rd ed. Honolulu: University of Hawaii Press.

Hunsberger, Bruce. 1995. "Religion and Prejudice: The Role of Religious Fundamentalism, Quest, and Right-Wing Authoritarianism." *Journal of Social Issues* 51: 113–129.

Hyde, Janet S., and Elizabeth A. Plant. 1995. "Magnitude of Psychological Gender Differences: Another Side to the Story." *American Psychologist* 30: 159–61.

Ifcic, Beverly L. 1993. *Values of Self-Direction/Conformity: Past and Present*. Master's thesis, Baylor University, Waco, TX.

Inglehart, Ronald. 1994. *Codebook for 1981–1984 and 1990–1993 World Values Survey*. Ann Arbor, MI: Inter-university Consortium for Political and Social Research.

————. 1990. *Cultural Shifts in Advanced Industrial Society*. Princeton, NJ: Princeton University Press.

Julian, Teresa W., Patrick C. McKenry, and Mary W. McKelvey. 1994. "Cultural Variations in Parenting: Perceptions of Caucasian, African-American, Hispanic, and Asian-American Parents." *Family Relations* 43: 30–37.

Kahle, Lynn R., and Susan Goff Timmer. 1983. "A Theory and a Method for Studying Values." Pp. 43-69 in *Social Values and Social Changes: Adaptation to Life in America*, edited by Lynn R. Kahle. New York: Praeger.

Kalleberg, Arne L. and James R. Lincoln. 1988. "The Structure of Earnings Inequality in the United States and Japan." *American Journal of Sociology* 94: 121–153.

Kalleberg, Arne L., and Barbara F. Reskin. 1995. "Gender Differences in Promotion in the United States and Norway." *Research in Social Stratification and Mobility* 14: 237–264.

Kay, Fiona M., and John Hagan. 1995. "The Persistent Glass Ceiling: Gendered Inequalities in the Earnings of Lawyers." *The British Journal of Sociology* 46: 279–310.

Kemp, Alice Abel. 1994. *Women's Work: Degraded and Devalued*. Englewood Cliffs, NJ: Prentice-Hall.

Kirkpatrick, Lee A. 1993. "Fundamentalism, Christian Orthodoxy, and Intrinsic Religious Orientation as Predictors of Discriminatory Attitudes." *Journal for the Scientific Study of Religion* 32: 256–268.

Kluckhohn, Clyde. 1951. "Values and Value Orientations in the Theory of Action: An Exploration in Definition and Classification." Pp. 388–433 in *Toward a General Theory of Action*, edited by Talcott Parsons and Edward Shils. Cambridge: Harvard University Press.

Kohn, Melvin L. 1977. *Class and Conformity: A Study in Values*, 2nd ed., Chicago: University of Chicago Press.

Kohn, Melvin L., Atsushi Naoi, Carrie Schoenbach, Carmi Schooler, and Kazimierz M. Slomczynski. 1990. "Position in the Class Structure and Psychological Functioning in the United States, Japan, and Poland." *American Journal of Sociology* 95: 964–1008.

Kohn, Melvin L., and Carmi Schooler. 1983. *Work and Personality: An Inquiry into the Impact of Social Stratification*. Norwood, NJ: Ablex.

Kohn, Melvin L., Kazimierz M. Slomczynski, and Carrie Schoenbach. 1986. "Social Stratification and the Transmission of Values in the Family: A Cross-National Assessment." *Sociological Forum* 1: 73–102.

Krosnick, Jon A. and Duane F. Alwin. 1988. "A Test of the Form-Resistant Correlation Hypothesis: Ratings, Rankings, and the Measurement of Values." *Public Opinion Quarterly* 52:526-538.

Kuo, Eddie C. Y. 1987. "Confucianism and the Chinese Family in Singapore: Continuities and Changes." Working Paper No. 83, Department of Sociology, National University of Singapore.

Lachmann, Richard. 1990. "Class Formation without Class Struggle: An Elite Conflict Theory of the Transition to Capitalism." *American Sociological Review* 55: 398–414.

Lee, Lee C., and Ginny Q. Zhan. 1991. "Political Socialization and Parental Values in the People's Republic of China." *International Journal of Behavioral Development* 14: 337–373.

Lenski, Gerhard. 1963. *The Religious Factor*. Garden City, NY: Doubleday.

Li, Qiang. 1994. "Occupational Structure of Contemporary Mainland China." *The Journal of East and West Studies* 23: 37–57.

Lin, Chin-Yau Cindy, and Victoria R. Fu. 1990. "A Comparison of Child-Rearing Practices among Chinese, Immigrant Chinese, and Caucasian-American Parents." *Child Development* 61: 429–433.

Lin, Nan and Yanjie Bian. 1991. "Getting ahead in Urban China." *American Journal of Sociology* 97: 657–688.

Linton, Ralph. 1945. *The Cultural Background of Personality*. New York: D. Apple-Century.

Lockwood, David. 1992. *Solidarity and Schism*. Oxford: Oxford University Press.

Lorr, Maurice. 1983. *Cluster Analysis for Social Scientists*. San Francisco: Jossey-Bass.

Luster, Tom, Kelly Rhoades, and Bruce Haas. 1989. "The Relation between Parental Values and Parenting Behavior: A Test of the Kohn Hypothesis." *Journal of Marriage and the Family* 51: 139–147.

Ma, Li-Chen, and Kevin Smith. 1993. "Education, Social Class, and Parental Values in Taiwan." *The Journal of Social Psychology* 133: 581–583.

Ma, Li-Chen, and Kevin Smith. 1990. "Social Class, Parental Values, and Child-Rearing Practices in Taiwan." *Sociological Spectrum* 10: 577–589.

Manion, Melanie. 1985. "The Cadre Management System, Post-Mao: The Appointment, Promotion, Transfer and Removal of Party and State Leaders." *China Quarterly* 102: 203–233.

Manly, Brian F. J. 1994. *Multivariate Statistical Methods*. London, U.K.: Chapman and Hall.

Margolis, Diane Rothbard. 1998. *The Fabric of Self*. New Haven, CT: Yale University Press.

Marini, Margaret Mooney. 1990. "Sex and Gender: What Do We Know?" *Sociological Forum* 5: 95–120.

Marini, Margaret Mooney, Pi-Ling Fan, Erica Finley, and Ann M. Beutel. 1996. "Gender and Job Values." *Sociology of Education* 69: 49–65.

Marx, Karl. [1894] 1977. *Capital*. Vol. 3. Pp. 488–507 in *Karl Marx: Selected Writings*, edited by David Mclellan. Oxford: Oxford University Press.

Mason, E. Sharon. 1994. "Work Values: A Gender Comparison and Implications for Practice." *Psychological Reports* 74: 415–418.

Miller, Alan S. and John P. Hoffmann. 1995. "Risk and Religion: An Explanation of Gender Differences in Religiosity." *Journal for the Scientific Study of Religion*. 34: 63–75.

Miller, Ann R., Donald J. Treiman, Pamela S. Cain, and Patricia Roos. 1980. *Work, Jobs, and Occupations: A Critical Review of the Dictionary of Occupational Titles*. Washington, DC: National Academy.

Miller, Daniel R., and Guy E. Swanson. 1958. *The Changing American Parent: A Study in the Detroit Area*. New York: John Wiley and Sons.

Miller, Joane, Carmi Schooler, Melvin L. Kohn, and Karen A. Miller. 1979. "Women and Work: The Psychological Effects of Occupational Conditions." *American Journal of Sociology* 85: 66–94.

Moghaddam, Fathali M., Donald M. Taylor, and Stephen C. Wright. 1993. *Social Psychology in Cross-Cultural Perspective*. New York: W. H. Freeman.

Morris, Charles William. 1956. *Variety of Human Values*. Chicago: University of Chicago Press.

Mortimer, Jeylan T. 1974. "Patterns of Intergenerational Occupational Movements: A Smallest-Space Analysis." *American Journal of Sociology* 79: 1278–1299.

Munro, Donald J. 1977. *The Concept of Man in Contemporary China*. Ann Arbor: University of Michigan Press.

Nan, Yan. 1998. "What Are the Family's Concerns?" Section 4 in *People's Daily* (Overseas Ed.).

Naoi, Michiko, and Carmi Schooler. 1985a. "Occupational Conditions and Psychological Functioning in Japan." *American Journal of Sociology* 90: 729–752.

Naoi, Michiko, and Carmi Schooler. 1985b. "Psychological Consequences of Occupational Conditions among Japanese Wives." *Social Psychology Quarterly* 58: 100–116.

Okin, Susan Moller. 1990. "Thinking like a Women." In *Theoretical Perspectives on Sexual Difference*, edited by Deborah Rhode. New Haven, CT: Yale University Press.

Olsen, Nancy J. 1975. "Social Class and Rural–Urban Patterns of Socialization in Taiwan." *Journal of Asian Studies* 34: 659–674.

Olsen, Nancy J. 1973. "Family Structure and Independence Training in a Taiwanese Village." *Journal of Marriage and the Family* 78: 512–519.

Opler, Marvin Kaufmann. 1967. *Culture and Social Psychiatry*. New York: Atherton Press.

Pan, Zhongdang, Steven H. Chaffee, Godwin C. Chu, and Yanan Ju. 1994. *To See Ourselves: Comparing Traditional Chinese and American Values.* Boulder, CO: Westview Press.

Pearlin, Leonard I., and Melvin L. Kohn. 1966. "Social Class, Occupation and Parental Values: A Cross-National Study." *American Sociological Review* 32: 466–479.

Peng, Yusheng. 1992. "Wage Determination in Rural and Urban China: A Comparison of Public and Private Industrial Sector." *American Sociological Review* 57: 198–213.

Peters, Marie Ferguson. 1988. "Parenting in Black Families with Young Children: A Historical Perspective." Pp. 228–241 in *Black Families*, 2nd ed., edited by Harriette Pipes McAdoo. Newbury Park, CA: Sage.

Prince-Gibson, Eetta, and Shalom H. Schwartz. 1998. "Value priorities and gender." *Social Psychology Quarterly* 61: 49–67.

Pye, Lucian W. 1984. *China*. Boston: Little, Brown and Company.

Redfield, Robert. 1953. *The Primitive World and Its Transformations*. Ithaca, NY: Cornell University Press.

Reskin, Barbara. 1988. "Bring the Men Back in: Sex Differentiation and the Devaluation of Women's Work." *Gender and Society* 2: 58–81.

Rokeach, Milton. 1973. *The Nature of Human Values*. New York: Free Press.

———. 1968. *Beliefs, Attitudes and Values*. San Francisco: Jossey-Bass.

Rokeach, Milton, and Sandra J. Ball-Rokeach. 1989. "Stability and Change in American Value Priorities, 1968–1981." *American Psychologist* 44: 775–784.

Rossi, Alice S., and Peter H. Rossi. 1991. *Of Human Bonding: Parent–Child Relations over the Life Course*. New York: Aldine de Gruyter.

Ruddick, Sara. 1989. *Maternal Thinking: Towards a Politics of Peace*. Boston: Beacon Press.

Sasaki, Masamichi, and Tatsuzo Suzuki. 1987. "Changes in Religious Commitment in the United States, Holland, and Japan." *American Journal of Sociology* 92: 1055–1076.

Schlozman, Kay Lehman, Nancy Burns, Sidney Verba, and Jesse Donahue. 1995. "Gender and Citizen Participation: Is There a Different Voice." *American Journal of Political Science* 39: 267–293.

Schwartz, Shalom H. 1992. "Universals in the Content and Structure of Values: Theoretical Advances and Empirical Tests in 20 Countries." Pp. 1–65 in *Advances in Experimental Social Psychology*, vol. 25, edited by Mark P. Zanna. Orlando: Academic Press.

Schwartz, Shalom H., and Spike Huismans. 1995. "Value Priorities and Religiosity in Four Western Religions." *Social Psychology Quarterly* 58: 88–107.

Shapiro, Robert Y., and Harpreet Mahajan. 1986. "Gender Differences in Policy Preferences: A Summary of Trends from the 1960's to the 1980's." *Public Opinion Quarterly* 50: 42–61.

Shields, Stephanie A., and Beth A. Koster. 1989. "Emotional Stereotyping in Childrearing Manuals, 1915–1980." *Social Psychology Quarterly* 52: 44–55.

Shryock, Henry S., Jacob S. Siegel, and Associates. 1992. *The Methods and Materials of Demography* (Condensed ed. by Edward G. Stockwell). San Diego: Academic Press.

Skolnick, Arlene S. 1991. *Embattled Paradise: The American Family in An Age of Uncertainty*. New York: Basic Books.

Slomczynski, Kazimierz M., Joanne Miller, and Melvin L. Kohn. 1981."Stratification, Work and Values." *American Sociological Review* 46: 720–744.

Smith, Peter B. and Michael Harris Bond. 1993. *Social Psychology across Cultures: Analysis and Perspectives*. London, U.K.: Harvester Wheatsheaf.

Smith, Peter B., Shaun Dugan, and Fons Trompenaars. 1996. "National Culture and the Values of Organizational Employees: A Dimensional Analysis Across 43 Nations." *Journal of Cross-Cultural Psychology* 27: 231–265.

Sochting, Ingrid, Eva E. Skoe, and James E. Marcia. 1994. "Care–Oriented Moral Reasoning and Prosocial Behavior: A Question of Gender or Sex Role Orientation." *Sex Roles* 31: 131–147.

Solomon, Richard H. 1965. "Educational Themes in China's Changing Culture." *China Quarterly* 21: 154–170.

Spade, Joan Z. 1994. "Wives' and Husbands' Perceptions of Why Wives Work." *Gender and Society* 8: 170–188.

Spade, Joan Z. 1991. "Occupational Structure and Men's and Women's Parental Values." *Journal of Family Issues* 12: 343–360.

Spence, Janet T. 1985. "Achievement American Style: The Rewards and Costs of Individualism." *American Psychologist* 40: 1285–1295.

Stacey, Judith. 1983. *Patriarchy and Socialist Revolution in China*. Berkeley: University of California Press.

Stander, Valerie, and Larry Jensen. 1993. "The Relationship of Value Orientation to Moral Cognition: Gender and Cultural Differences in the United States and China Explored." *Journal of Cross-Cultural Psychology* 24: 42–52.

Szelényi, Iván. 1978. "Social Inequality in State Socialist Redistributive Economies." *International Journal of Comparative Sociology* 19: 63–97.

Thomas, Robert. 1993. *What Machines Can't Do*. Berkeley: University of California Press.

Thomson, Elizabeth, Sara S. McLanahan, and Roberta Braun Curtin. 1992. "Family Structure, Gender, and Parental Socialization." *Journal of Marriage and the Family* 54, 845–871.

Triandis, Harry Charalambos. 1995. *Individualism and Collectivism*. Boulder, CO: Westview Press.

Tu, Wei-ming. 1993. "Confucianism." Pp. 139–227 in *Our Religions,* edited by Arvind Sharma. New York: HarperCollins.

———. 1990. "The Confucian Tradition in Chinese History." Pp. 112–137 in *Heritage of China: Contemporary Perspectives on Chinese Civilization,*" edited by Paul S. Ropp. Berkeley: University of California Press.

U.S. Department of Commerce, Bureau of the Census. 1990. *Statistical Abstract of the United States.* Washington, DC: Bureau of the Census.

Vaux, A. 1985. "Variations in Social Support Associated with Gender, Ethnicity, and Age." *Journal of Social Issues* 41: 89–110.

Walder, Andrew G. 1995. "Career Mobility and the Communist Political Order." *American Sociological Review* 60: 309–328.

———. 1992. "Property Rights and Stratification in Socialist Redistributive Economies." *American Sociological Review* 57: 524–539.

———. 1985. "The Political Dimension of Social Mobility in Communist States: China and Soviet Union." *Research in Political Sociology* 1: 101–117.

Walker, L. 1986. "Experiential and Cognitive Sources of Moral Development in Adulthood." *Human Development* 29: 113–124.

———. 1984. "Sex Differences in the Development of Moral Reasoning: A Critical Review." *Child Development* 55: 677–691.

Wang, Y. L. 1990. "Changes in Urban Women's Double Roles and Their Families." *Sociological Studies* 4: 22–23.

Wang, Y., and J. Li. 1982. "Urban Workers' Housework." *Social Sciences in China* 3: 147–165.

Warner, R. Stephen. 1993. "Work in Progress toward a New Paradigm for the Sociological Study of Religion in the United States." *American Journal of Sociology* 98: 1044–1093.

Weber, Max. 1946. "Class, Status, Party." Pp. 180–195 in *Max Weber: Essays in Sociology,* translated by Hans H. Gerth and C. Write Mills. New York: Oxford University Press.

West, Candace, and Don Zimmerman. 1987. "Doing Gender." *Gender and Society* 1: 125–151.

Wilkie, Jane Riblett. 1993. "Changes in U.S. Men's Attitudes toward the Family Provider Role, 1972–1989." *Gender and Society* 7: 261–279.

Williams, Robin M., Jr. 1970. *American Society: A Sociological Interpretation.* 3rd ed. New York: Alfred A. Knopf.

World Values Study Group. 1994. *World Values Survey, 1981–1984 and 1990–1993* [Computer file]. ICPSR version. Ann Arbor, MI: Institute for Social Research [producer]. Ann Arbor, MI: Inter-university Consortium for Political and Social Research [distributor].

Wright, Erik Olin. 1985. *Classes.* London: New Left.

———. 1976. "Class Boundaries in Advanced Capitalist Societies." *New Left Review* 98: 3–41.

Wright, James D., and Sonia R. Wright. 1976. "Social Class and Parental Values for Children: A Partial Replication and Extension of the Kohn Thesis." *American Sociological Review* 41: 527–537.

Wu, David Y. H.,and Wen-Shing Tseng. 1985. "Introduction: The Characteristics of Chinese Culture." Pp. 3–13 in *Chinese Culture and Mental Health*, edited by Wen-Shing Tseng and David Y. H. Wu. Orlando: Academic Press.

Xiao, Hong, and Nancy Andes. 1999. "Sources of Parental Values." *Journal of Human Values* 5: 157–167.

Xie, Qing, and Francine Hultgren. 1994. "Urban Chinese Parents' Perceptions of Their Strengths and Needs in Rearing 'Only' Sons and Daughters." *Home Economic Research Journals* 22: 340–56.

Xie, Yu, and Emily Hannum. 1996. "Regional Variation in Earnings Inequality in Reform-Era Urban China." *American Journal of Sociology* 101: 950–92.

Yamagata, Hisashi, Kuang S. Yeh, Shelby Stewman, and Hiroko Dodge. 1997. "Sex Segregation and Glass Ceilings: A Comparative Statistical Model of Women's Career Opportunities in the Federal Government over a Quarter Century." *American Journal of Sociology* 103: 566–632.

Zhou, Xueguang, Nancy Brandon Tuma, and Phyllis Moen. 1996. "Stratification Dynamics under State Socialism: The Case of Urban China, 1949–1993." *Social Forces* 74: 759–796.

Index

About the Author

HONG XIAO is Assistant Professor of Sociology at Central Washington University. Professor Xiao's earlier writings appear in *Gender & Society*, *Sociological Quarterly*, and *Journal of Comparative Family Studies*.